The
Immigrant
EXODUS

The
Immigrant
EXODUS

Why America Is Losing the Global Race to Capture Entrepreneurial Talent

VIVEK WADHWA
with Alex Salkever

DIGITAL PRESS
Philadelphia

© 2012 by Vivek Wadhwa

Published by Wharton Digital Press
The Wharton School
University of Pennsylvania
3620 Locust Walk
2000 Steinberg Hall-Dietrich Hall
Philadelphia, PA 19104
Email: whartondigitalpress@gmail.com
Website: http://wdp.wharton.upenn.edu

Ebook ISBN: 978-1-61363-020-4
Paperback ISBN: 978-1-61363-021-1

Acknowledgments

First and foremost, this book is dedicated to the United States of America—the country that readily embraces people like myself who speak with foreign accents, look different, think different, sometimes dress different, and challenge its natives to work harder and think smarter.

I want to thank my wife, Tavinder, for her patience and sensibility and for always being there for me, and my sons, Vineet and Tarun, for being my best friends and my strongest critics. I would also like to thank my many bosses, colleagues, and students at all the different universities that have supported me and my research, including Tom Katsouleas, Barry Myers, Peter Lange, Kristina Johnson, Gary Gereffi, Ben Rissing, Jeff Glass, and Brad Fox of Duke University; Richard Freeman, Elaine Bernardt, and John Trumpbour of Harvard University; AnnaLee Saxenian of the University of California, Berkeley; Larry Kramer, Dan Siciliano, and Joe Grundfest of Stanford University; Holli Semetko and Benn Konsynski of Emory University; and Peter Diamandis, Ray Kurzweil, Naveen Jain, and Rob Nail of Singularity University. The students are too numerous to name. You will find them on the covers of my research papers. For the latest research that led to this book, I want to thank Neesha Bapat for cracking the whip and getting the data ready on time.

Thanks to the Kauffman Foundation for enabling me to do such extensive research into entrepreneurship and immigration.

The foundation has provided far more than funding: Bob Litan, Lesa Mitchell, Carl Schramm, Dane Stangler, and Wendy Guillies have been friends and guides.

And thanks to my friend Alex Salkever for helping me write this book. And thank you to my childhood friend John Harvey, who drives me crazy with his perfectionist edits to my writing.

Contents

Introduction

On a bright sunny day in February 2012, I sat on a stage at an awards ceremony at NASA's Moffett Field in Silicon Valley. Tremendous pride and gratitude welled up inside me. I was one of five distinguished recipients of the Outstanding American by Choice award that day. The annual award recognizes outstanding entrepreneurs, scientists, and business leaders who have immigrated to the United States and chosen to become citizens of this great land. Other recipients that day included Sequoia Capital managing partner Michael Moritz and Menlo Ventures managing director Shervin Pishevar, two of Silicon Valley's most respected venture capitalists, and entrepreneurs Ping Fu and Christopher Che.

We all shook the hand of Alejandro Mayorkas, the director of US Citizenship and Immigration Services (USCIS). I knew that the award was both an honor and an irony, given my vocal criticisms of US immigration policy. When I got word of my award, Mayorkas told me that the government appreciated all my efforts to make the country more competitive and that my criticisms of his department had motivated his team to work harder to improve the system. And that was why I had received the award, as strange as it sounds.

I didn't start as a critic. I came to America at age six and fell in love with the country.

In 1963, my father was posted to the Indian consulate in New York City. I loved New York—the tall buildings, the museums, and all the comings and goings that make the Big Apple feel like the center of the known universe. I also fell in love with the American people. They were kind and open-minded.

There was a strong sense of patriotism that I had never felt before. When an assassin killed President John F. Kennedy during my first year in America, my family and I grieved with the rest of the country and shared in the collective sense of loss. True, we faced some discrimination. Americans thought India was a nation of cow worshippers. Children taunted me and asked if I charmed snakes. At first I used to cry. Then I learned to smile and explain that not everyone in India was like that. Most of the children listened. Many of them became my friends. Neither they nor their parents knew of India's long history of scholarship, its great civilizations, or its many significant contributions, such as the first use of zero and construction of the Taj Mahal.

When I was ten, my father's post ended, and I left America reluctantly, hopeful that I might one day return. As a teenager, I went to Canberra, Australia, for my undergraduate studies. The University of Canberra offered one of the world's first computer science degrees. A friend had introduced me to computers, punch cards, and writing code. I decided that I wanted to work with computers for my career and began spending copious amounts of time in the computing lab.

Even then, computer programmers were in high demand. Immediately after graduation, I received a good job and permanent residency in Australia. I was about to accept Australian citizenship and anticipated spending the rest of my life in my new country. Then, in January 1980, my father called to say he was being transferred back to the United States as a delegate to the United Nations and that I could join him on a diplomatic visa. I jumped at this chance, immediately resigning from my job, packing my bags, and buying a one-way ticket. I didn't think twice about leaving a secure place in Australia, because I knew great things were possible in America.

Part of my decision, of course, related to computer science. Back then, the United States was the only real destination for someone serious about information technology. Within days of my arrival, I applied for and received a job at the Xerox Corporation. It was a lowly entry-level programmer job in the publishing division. But Xerox was considered one of the most innovative companies in the world and a place where cutting-edge technology was developed. I knew about Xerox's Palo Alto Research Center (PARC), where the mouse, the graphical user interface, and other famous inventions were developed. And I was thrilled to be working for a company on the bleeding edge of computer science.

A mere 18 months after I had started at Xerox, I obtained my green card (which is the common name for a permanent residency visa). Xerox sponsored my candidacy, and the process was painless. Although I was still a few years away from legal citizenship, I became an American in my heart the day my permanent residence papers arrived in the mail. Six years after starting at Xerox, I moved up to a more senior programmer-analyst job at a leading Wall Street bank, First Boston (which later became Credit Suisse First Boston). It was an exciting time. First Boston had decided to bet its future on a new type of computing architecture called "client-server."

The sea change in information systems we proposed—moving away from massive mainframe-driven coding to more distributed code running in smaller systems—was controversial and very risky. Lots of people said we would fail and this would jeopardize First Boston's survival. Sometimes I, too, worried that we might fail. But we succeeded, and I found the process of creating new technologies exhilarating and fulfilling.

Despite this success, I wanted more. I wanted our technology to have an impact on the world. Other companies were watching us with great interest. They had asked about our technology, and First Boston managing director Gene Bedell saw an opportunity to create a spin-off company. We would, however, have to leave the security of First Boston and risk it all in a small startup. This type of talk made my wife, Tavinder, nervous. In those days, Wall Street was synonymous with security, and the salaries were as stratospheric as those you read about today. I could always get a good job in an executive suite somewhere. Why rock the boat, possibly burn bridges, and take a huge pay cut? In less than a decade, we had gone from struggling to wealthy. We had two young boys to raise and nurture. Tavinder was worried about the risk.

But technology was my baby, too. I wanted to help it grow up and allow others to use it to do good for the world. Tavinder, ever patient and understanding, said she would support me in anything I did. Bedell was a great salesperson and convinced me that this was a once-in-a-lifetime opportunity. International Business Machines (IBM) saw our technology as something it could use internally and sell to clients. So I took the leap and became the executive vice president and chief technology officer of Seer Technologies, bringing my development team from First Boston. Our beginnings were unusual. IBM—the technology company—invested the capital. First Boston—the bank—provided the technology. We grew revenue from nothing to a profitable $120 million in just five years and notched a successful initial public offering (IPO). Back then the company was valued at more than $300 million, a solid midcap valuation. Seer was one of the fastest-growing software companies of its time. We created 1,000 well-paying jobs and served as a breeding ground for numerous technology spin-offs launched by our alumni.

My second startup, Relativity Technologies, didn't grow big enough to get to an IPO, but it did create more than 200 well-paying jobs, mostly in North Carolina. We were one of the leading technology innovators in the Research Triangle Park area. As the founder and chief executive officer (CEO), I raised more than $20 million in venture capital and helped the US Air Force and blue-chip American companies such as Charles Schwab, Fidelity Investments, and Citibank quickly and easily modernize their computer systems by moving them from old computing platforms to newer ones. At Relativity, I navigated the company through the dot-com crash and many other challenges. I worked too hard and burned myself out.

In March 2002, at the end of my first vacation in two years—a cruise to Mexico—I had a massive heart attack. I started having frequent chest and back pains while on the cruise. I ignored these pains because I thought I was indestructible. As our flight was landing in Raleigh, North Carolina, I felt a shooting pain in my left arm. My wife drove me straight to the hospital. Doctors performed an EKG and immediately admitted me for an emergency cardiac procedure. They said that if I had come in two hours later, I never would have checked out of the hospital; I would have ended up in the morgue instead. I spent three days in critical care. Tavinder stayed by my side day and night. She didn't sleep—she wouldn't let me die.

Back to School

After my heart attack, Tavinder put her foot down and said she would not let me get back to the rough-and-tough technology world. Life is short, she said. We would make do with less. Do something less stressful that feeds your soul, she insisted. I agreed. But I could not retire. Seer Technologies stock had soared and then crashed during the 1990s. I had not sold my shares because I did not want to cash in while our shareholders were losing their shirts. So I never made the big millions. Fortunately, we did have enough in savings for me to take a few years off and do something different. Tavinder suggested I do what I had always dreamed about: become a professor and teach. I had taught many classes as a guest lecturer, and I loved the interaction with smart young minds. I felt I had learned a lot in my career and was eager to share. What better way to give back to the country that had done so much for me?

I took a position at Duke University's Pratt School of Engineering as an adjunct professor and executive in residence. I taught entrepreneurship but quickly realized that I would need to perform original research. I chose to study globalization and innovation. India and China were transforming from economic backwaters to technology powerhouses. Both aspired to challenge the United States for technology leadership. After researching this shift in geotechnological power, I decided I would investigate America's advantages and brainstorm policies to keep our country on top.

As an entrepreneur, I became aware of how many Indian and Chinese immigrants started technology companies. The number seemed way out of proportion to their representation in the US population. It turned out that a scholar had made the same observation several years before I did. A University of California, Berkeley, professor, AnnaLee Saxenian, had performed the first deep-dive analysis of Silicon Valley's skilled immigrants, publishing a report titled "Silicon Valley's New Immigrant Entrepreneurs." She found that in 1998 Indian and Chinese computer scientists and engineers ran about one-quarter of the region's high-tech companies. Those companies accounted for more than 58,000 jobs and nearly $17 billion in sales.[1] I contacted Saxenian to ask if we could jointly update her research and expand it to a national level. She agreed.

Together we surveyed more than 2,000 high-tech entrepreneurs, compiling our results in a report titled "America's New Immigrant Entrepreneurs," which would become the first of a series. We discovered that the trend she first documented had accelerated and expanded. From 1995 to 2005, more than 25% of all the technology and engineering companies in the country had one or more immigrant founders. The proportion of technology and engineering companies in Silicon Valley with at least one immigrant founder was 52%. We were also surprised to learn that within a decade the proportion of Indian-led startups had increased from 7% to 13.4%.[2] Skilled immigrants were coming to America en masse, starting companies and creating quality jobs.

I began reaching out to these entrepreneurs, asking them how public policy could support their investment in the United States. A growing number complained about the waiting period for green cards. The wait had grown from one year in my time to three, then five, then ten years. Although the US government had raised the quota for H-1B visas for highly skilled workers, the quota for employment-based green cards remained the same, leaving many in an immigration limbo. What's more, the green card award system mandated that no country obtain more than 7% of the total pool. Chinese and Indian engineers dominated the ranks of H-1B visa holders, creating a mismatch between allowable quotas and the best and brightest skilled immigrants. People who entered on high-skilled H-1B visas were stuck with their sponsoring company, unable to switch jobs unless they could secure another sponsor. H-1B holders could not leave to launch a startup. And their spouses on H-4 visas could not work in America under any circumstances.

All of this was happening as the economies of countries like India and China were growing rapidly. These skilled workers now had the option of returning home to business and career opportunities that were often better than those available to them in the United States. So why would they put up with the frustrations of waiting a decade or longer for a green card? Many didn't care about public policy; they said they were headed home to greener pastures.

I also interviewed hundreds of smart, talented technology entrepreneurs from Brazil, China, England, France, India, New Zealand, and other countries who wanted to launch ventures in the United States. Immigration officials had denied their visas. In fact, there was no differentiated status for startups aside from the existing EB-5 visa class, which required significant capital investments to obtain the right to work in America. Most of these startups were still seeking capital, so they were out of luck. Many of these founders who came and then left said they had made the right choice. Those from China and India in particular said they were pleasantly surprised to find a healthy startup ecosystem thriving back home, including a budding homegrown venture capital sector.

I learned America was also losing its allure among foreign students. After the September 11, 2001, attacks, it became markedly harder to get a visa. That condition has since been reversed, but a surprising number of the foreign students who came after 9/11 have said they do not want to stay permanently in the United States. Many believed their home countries offered better economic opportunities in the long term. This was particularly true for Indian and Chinese students. Even though nearly all of these students said they would love to stay and work in the United States for a few years, they would rather ultimately return home to their family and friends. Among these students, too, many expressed concerns about obtaining a US work visa, something that had become incredibly competitive due to the rabid appetite for H-1B visa status workers from major multinational technology and financial companies.

During the spring and summer of 2012, I conducted a follow-up survey, with Saxenian and F. Daniel Siciliano of Stanford Law School, to tabulate the percentage of technology and engineering startups with immigrant founders and see what changes had occurred since our previous survey seven years earlier. The new data from this study show that what had been a fast-rising tide of immigrant-led startups in the United States has slowed and reversed to an Immigrant Exodus. In Silicon Valley and the rest of the country, the percentage of high-growth startups with immigrant founders is in decline. This is unprecedented.

In my previous survey of immigrant entrepreneurs, "Education, Entrepreneurship and Immigration," I found the median time they spent in the United States before launching their first tech startup was 13 years.[3] Given the influx of entrepreneurs on H-1B visas in the late 1990s and early 2000s, the proportion of immigrant-founded startups should have increased correspondingly 12 to 15 years after this influx. The stagnation and drop in startup formation is cause for serious alarm.

If the conditions were as they are today when I started my own path to citizenship, I would have been a fool to leave Australia. If I had landed in the United States on an H-1B visa today, my wait for a green card could be a decade or longer. I would be stuck in the same low-level position and prevented from seizing opportunities for personal growth. I would not be creating jobs for others either. If my company got into financial trouble and laid me off, I would have to depart the United States immediately. No matter how long you have worked in the United States, you are illegal the day after your job ends.

My family would also be held hostage to my immigration status. My wife would not have been able to work. Depending on the state where we lived, she would not even be able to get a driver's license or open a bank account. We would not have risked buying a house. My American-born children would have been entitled to US citizenship. But if I had had to leave, they would have had to choose between their country and their father.

My participation and investment in my community would have been significantly diminished. Due to my constant awareness that I could be kicked out without notice, I would not have considered the local community as my own. I would have been less likely to mentor students or give volunteer presentations. My companies—Seer Technologies and Relativity Technologies— would never have been formed. My most productive years would have been wasted in worries and making do, rather than changing the world. And in due time, I would have been miserable. Such is the plight of today's skilled immigrant entrepreneurs.

The Immigrant Exodus

The American Dream I knew is losing its luster. Restrictive US immigration policies and the rise of other countries' economies are driving talent elsewhere.

When I immigrated here, America was the only viable destination for serious technology entrepreneurs. Standouts in science, engineering, technology, and mathematics research flocked here, too. Now more than ever before, the United States needs immigrant entrepreneurs to retain its competitive edge. But now these entrepreneurs need America less than ever before.

The trend has become so common that it has a name: the reverse brain drain. At almost every entrepreneurship event in Silicon Valley, I meet skilled immigrants on temporary visas who have great ideas but can't start companies because of their visa restrictions. Visit Bangalore, Shanghai, São Paulo, or any other big city in India, China, or Brazil, and you will find hundreds of innovative startups founded by people trained in US schools and companies.

In addition, the competition has gotten stiffer. Many countries, including Australia, Canada, Chile, China, and Singapore, recognize the opportunity in attracting entrepreneurs, technologists, and other skilled workers. These countries are offering stipends, labor subsidies for employees, expedited visa processes, and other inducements to bring in startups. As a result of these aggressive recruitment policies, hundreds, if not thousands, of startup companies that might have launched in America are now taking root elsewhere.

Take the case of Jason Gang Jin. After holding prestigious positions in the United States at top-level academic institutions such as the Salk Institute for Biological Studies, Jin could have stayed in the United States and waited to become a citizen. Instead he chose to return to his native China to launch Shanghai Biochip, now one of the leading genomics library and biotech drug research companies in Asia. The Chinese government offered him a generous package of subsidies to help start his company there.

The irony is that the majority of these skilled immigrants and the thousands of startup founders who have been barred from getting a visa remain intent on obtaining one. Despite treatment from the US government that many I spoke with called "insulting" or "humiliating," most remained willing to go through great effort and expense in this quest for the opportunity to legally work and build a company in America. For example, Mayel de Borniol tried to launch his company, Babelverse, in Chile after US immigration policies forced him out. The crowd-sourced translation company was selected as a winner at a major technology conference and received offers of significant funding. De Borniol is still fighting to get a visa that will allow him to work and build his startup in the United States. Immigrants Anand and Shikha Chhatpar built a burgeoning Facebook games company in the United States. Immigration officials unexpectedly forced them out in 2010. They hired programmers in India instead of in Silicon Valley to build their next startup. Despite this rough treatment they, too, wish to return to the United States, and they have engaged a US attorney to help their chances with USCIS.

This shows that the United States can quickly halt the Immigrant Exodus. Simple, direct, and obvious changes to our existing immigration laws and policies can stop the entrepreneur and talent shift and secure America's place as the world leader in innovation. And it wouldn't cost US taxpayers a dime. It would deliver billions of dollars in taxes into the US Treasury, drive a renewal in US hegemony over global patent filings, and create new jobs at the scale we need in order to revive our economy.

In This Book

In the following chapters, I analyze the crisis in detail and propose how we can reverse the course of the Immigrant Exodus. In chapter 1, I illustrate the importance of immigrants to US job growth and economic development, particularly in technology sectors. I also show immigrants' critical role in intellectual capital formation in America. In chapter 2, I provide a history of the rise and decline of the immigrant-powered startup machine in America. In chapter 3, I discuss why immigrants are leaving the United States and detail the many attractive options they are enjoying elsewhere. In chapter 4, I explain why the H-1B visa system is horribly broken and the effect this has had on skilled immigrants. In chapter 5, I provide insights into the rest of the world's attempts to replicate the success of Silicon Valley and recruit the best global talent. In chapter 6, I lay out seven fixes that, collectively, would reverse the Immigrant Exodus nearly instantaneously and help boost the US economy.

My Commitment

When I was named an Outstanding American by Choice, the US government was honoring me for my "commitment to this country and to the common civic values that unite us as Americans." The phone call from Mayorkas telling me I had won the award brought tears to my eyes. This is the greatness of America and why this country leads the world: Disagreement and debate are cherished.

Even though the United States is facing many problems when it comes to attracting and retaining skilled immigrants, the United States remains the most entrepreneurial, technologically advanced society on earth. How long the United States can hold onto this leading role is, for the first time, a subject of open debate. As part of my commitment to this country, I offer *The Immigrant Exodus* as a concise framework for understanding our crisis and a recipe for reversal and rapid recovery. We cannot wait any longer to fix this problem. The future of America depends on it.

CHAPTER 1

Why the Future of America Depends on Skilled Immigrants

A s an undergraduate studying at Government Polytechnic, Mumbai, Anand Chhatpar launched his first software company, Pyxoft Infotech. After graduating at the top of his class with a degree in computer engineering, Chhatpar entered the University of Wisconsin–Madison in 2001. At his new school, he immersed himself in the culture of startups, entering business plan competitions and collaborating with fellow students and professors to brainstorm business ideas. He interned with Pitney Bowes and other organizations, garnering eight utility patents from the US Patent and Trademark Office.

During his junior year, Chhatpar founded BrainReactions with two other students. The company provided a platform to harness undergraduate insights to help large corporations solve problems and innovate. The business served dozens of notable clients such as Bank of America, Black & Decker, BMW, General Mills, Intuit, Kellogg's, Procter & Gamble, and the United Nations. Chhatpar ran the business while pulling a 3.978 GPA in computer engineering.

Anand met Shikha at the University of Wisconsin–Madison and married her in November 2008. Just after she graduated, the Chhatpars launched another business, Fame Express, in order to build Facebook game applications. The company's apps were played online by 20 million people around the world and garnered 900,000 fans. In the first two years alone, Fame Express grossed about $1 million, and the Chhatpars paid more than

$250,000 in taxes. Anand carved out a media profile, appearing in numerous media outlets including CNBC, *US News & World Report*, and the *Los Angeles Times*. In September 2010, the Chhatpars returned to India for a legally mandated period, while awaiting paperwork from the US Citizenship and Immigration Service (USCIS) that would clear a path to citizenship.

The Economic Impact

The US economy has benefited tremendously from people like the Chhatpars, who have come to this county, started businesses, and created new jobs. Few dispute that since the inception of this nation, immigration has driven significant economic growth. Many of the United States' greatest entrepreneurs and business leaders were first- or second-generation immigrants. This has been true since the founding of the United States as a nation composed of people seeking better economic chances and religious freedom in the New World, a process that started with the arrival of the Mayflower.

Each decade has yielded top-flight entrepreneurs not born in this land, from Andrew Carnegie (Carnegie Steel Company) to Alexander Graham Bell (AT&T) to Charles Pfizer (Pfizer) to Vinod Khosla (Sun Microsystems) to Sergey Brin (Google) to Elon Musk (PayPal, SpaceX, Tesla Motors). A 2011 study by the Partnership for a New American Economy tabulated that first-generation immigrants or their children had founder roles in more than 40% of the Fortune 500. These companies had combined revenues of greater than $4.2 trillion and employed more than 10 million workers worldwide.[4]

More and more evidence indicates that immigrant founders drive a wildly disproportionate percentage of all net new job creation in America. An analysis of 2010 US Census data (the American Community Survey) by the Fiscal Policy Institute found that immigrants constituted 12% of small business owners in this country in 1990 and 18% in 2010, a 50% increase.[5] Small businesses drive new job creation. Immigrants start companies, and every startup begins its life as a small business. According to the Bureau of Labor Statistics, new businesses account for 65% of all net new jobs in America. The US Bureau of the Census puts that number even higher, at 90% of all net new jobs.[6] According to "Open for Business," a 2012 report by the Partnership for a New American Economy, immigrants are more than twice as likely as native-born Americans to start a business. Immigrants, the report further found, "were responsible for more than one in every four (28%) US businesses founded in 2011, significantly outpacing their share of the population (12.9%).[7] Thus, net new job creation—the most important economic driver of the US economy—has become inextricably linked to and dependent upon immigration and the skills of immigrants.

Immigrants occupy founding or key managerial roles in the highest-impact startups at a rate far disproportionate to their share of the US population. A 2011 National Foundation for American Policy (NFAP) study of founding and management teams at the Top 50 venture-backed companies in the United States, as ranked by VentureSource, found that immigrants started nearly half of America's 50 top venture-funded companies and are key members of management or product development teams in more than 75% of those companies.[8] One of those companies, social enterprise communication tools company Yammer, was purchased by Microsoft for $1.2 billion in June 2012.[9] The crucial role of immigrant founders in the enormous success of US technology concerns continues all the way to the pinnacle of job growth and value creation: the initial public offering. According to the aforementioned NFAP study, 25% of the publicly traded companies created between 1990 and 2005 that had received venture backing also had immigrant founders.[10]

The Innovation Impact

Sophie Vandebroek is the chief technology officer and president of the Innovation Group at Xerox. She was born in Leuven, Belgium, earned a master's degree in electromechanical engineering from Katholieke Universiteit Leuven, and immigrated to the United States in 1986. Her husband, who accompanied her, had also earned a master's degree in electromechanical engineering from the same university and later completed a master of business administration (MBA) at Cornell University. His company, a medium-size firm in Rochester, New York, wanted to sponsor him for a green card but couldn't because he didn't have a PhD.

In 1990, as she was completing her PhD in electrical engineering from Cornell, Vandebroek joined a large multinational near New York City. She commuted 300 miles to work even though she had two children at home. But she became frustrated that the company would not file for her green card. Vandebroek explains, "The approach my company took with foreign students was to wait as long as possible to get them their green card." So she resigned and joined Xerox in 1991. As it did for me, Xerox immediately sponsored her for a green card, and she received it within 18 months.

Two decades later, Vandebroek is head of all of Xerox's research laboratories around the globe. She has received 12 patents, been inducted into the Women in Technology Hall of Fame, and become a fellow at the Institute of Electrical and Electronics Engineers (IEEE).

At companies such as Xerox, the most prized employees in research and development (R&D) provide breakthroughs that are so unique and defensible that they merit patent awards. For the past 60 years, the United States has dominated global patent filings. Skilled immigrants, often on H-1B visas, have contributed mightily to this supremacy. Patent filing statistics provide the proof. Patent filings are a generally accepted proxy for science and technology innovation, which is why my team decided to perform an analysis of the World Intellectual Property Organization (WIPO) database in 2007 for what would become our initial report, "America's New Immigrant Entrepreneurs." We found that the number of international patent applications filed by noncitizen immigrants increased from 7.3% in 1998 to 24.2% in 2006.[11] Among foreign-born patent holders, those from China (Mainland and Taiwan) made up the largest group. Indian nationals were second, followed by Canadians and the British, respectively.[12]

Even that tally likely understates the contributions of immigrants. The WIPO database records nationality at time of filing. Many of the recipients who were US citizens were probably not native born and had immigrated after undergraduate, graduate, or postgraduate education in the United States. For example, during the period covered by my research, I coauthored two patents. But I was not included in the immigrant count—I was a US citizen when these were filed.

Other research echoes our findings. A June 2012 report by the Partnership for a New American Economy found that 76% of the patents awarded to the top patent-producing universities in 2011 had at least one foreign-born inventor.[13] Those foreign-born inventors "played especially large roles in cutting-edge fields like semiconductor device manufacturing (87%), information technology (84%), pulse or digital communications (83%), pharmaceutical drugs or drug compounds (79%), and optics (77%)."[14]

The enterprise of skilled immigrants has gone beyond universities and benefited US-based multinational corporations. In our 2007 report "Intellectual Property, the Immigration Backlog, and a Reverse Brain-Drain," we explain that foreign nationals and foreign residents contributed to more than half of the international patents filed by a number of large, multinational companies, including Qualcomm (72%), Merck (65%), General Electric (64%), Siemens (63%), and Cisco (60%).[15]

US patents, too, are increasingly dominated by applications from foreigners. According to the US Patent and Trademark Office website, the percentage of total US patent grants to foreigners has nearly tripled, rising from 18% in 1964 to 51% in 2011.[16] However, this patent dominance is waning. From 1995 to 2010, the US country share of total patent filings with the WIPO declined from 42.8% to 27.4%.[17]

What would the world look like if more and more foreign nationals and foreign residents who in the past might have filed patents in the United States instead were filing patents in India or China on behalf of Indian or Chinese companies? How long would it take for the global balance of technology power to shift? How long would it take for those contributions to elevate China and India to the same status as the United States? We don't know the answers to these questions, but we may be perilously close to finding out as these innovators and entrepreneurs leave at a hastening clip.

So for all intents and purposes, the debate about whether immigrants drive company formation and job growth in America is over. The evidence is overwhelming. We need immigrants to drive job growth. We need skilled immigrants to drive technology job growth. We need immigrants to drive technology innovation in America and maintain this country's lead in the global race for technological supremacy.

The Shifting Tide

Two months after the Chhatpars returned to India for the legally mandated period, their petition for EB-1 status was denied, despite the fact that they already had employees in the United States, were paying considerable taxes in the United States, had a clear track record of starting companies, and BusinessWeek. com had once featured Anand as one of the "Best Entrepreneurs Under 25."[18]

Obviously, this type of purgatory is bad for business. Says Anand, "Now, after returning to India because of the denial of both our petitions, running our companies (both registered in the United States) has become extremely difficult. As a result, our companies are suffering. Our tax returns can prove that we weren't able to make profits since moving to India and haven't contributed a single dollar to the IRS since then." (Full disclosure—I brought his situation to the attention of Alejandro Mayorkas in May 2012, and he said he would "forward this communication to the appropriate individuals in our agency for consideration as to how best to proceed.")

Today, the Chhatpars are living in Bangalore running both Fame Express and BrainReactions. They have hired four computer programmers to develop India-focused websites. They would rather be working on products for the US market, but given their immigration uncertainties, they feel they have no other choice. And, in all likelihood, some of those jobs would have gone to US-based programmers had the United States not ousted the Chhatpars.

For her part, Vandebroek says she can't imagine leaving the United States. But she sees other top researchers packing up. Recently, two of her top PhDs resigned from the Xerox research center in Webster, New York, to take academic positions in

South Korea. One is married to another PhD researcher at the Webster research lab, so that totals three losses for Xerox. These are just the most recent losses. Vandebroek says that over the past five years there have been many others. America's loss has been the gain of countries such as India, China, and Korea.

Vandebroek says, "Clearly the attraction the United States had on people like myself two to three decades ago is very different now. Countries all over the globe now have successful and growing research universities and labs. It is critical that the US figure out how to encourage bright and passionate scientists and engineers to immigrate to the US and contribute to a better future for all of us." And, in truth, Vandebroek, too, might have left those many years ago had she been forced to wait longer for a green card and put her family through continued stress and uncertainty.

So how did we get here? In the next chapter, I look at what has happened in Silicon Valley to explore how the United States has gone from the uncontested leader in acquiring the best global talent to facing serious competition. Once a destination of unparalleled attraction for the world's smartest engineers and technologists, the leading global tech center is rapidly losing its luster for this precious class of innovators.

CHAPTER 2

The Rise and Decline of the Immigrant-Powered Startup Machine

If you are Chinese and want to book travel online, chances are you use Ctrip. The largest online travel company in the Middle Kingdom, Ctrip is one of the breakout successes of the Chinese Internet, going on to make an IPO on the Nasdaq stock exchange. Although Ctrip nailed the China travel market, the company benefited from a founding team with deep experience in Silicon Valley. James Liang, one of the company's cofounders, served as CEO from 2000 to 2006. He is presently the chairman of Ctrip's board of directors. Before founding Ctrip with three others in 1999, Liang studied at the Georgia Institute of Technology and worked in the United States and China for eight years at the database giant Oracle.

Liang ultimately rose to the head of Oracle's Enterprise Resource Planning consulting division for China, a prestigious post that positioned him for a top executive position in the company. Rather than remain in the Oracle fold or launch a startup in Silicon Valley, Liang chose to build his business in China. People like Liang—expats who return home—are called "sea turtles" in China. Generally people of strong capabilities and skills, they could have remained in the West but chose to return to the East in search of better opportunities. This marks a historical sea change. Since the dawn of the technology era, the tide has flowed the other way.

Starting in 1965, thousands of Indian and Chinese foreign students who had stayed in the United States, and others who had managed to emigrate, moved to the San Francisco Bay Area to work in fast-growing technology enterprises and the research labs that sprung up to feed them. Prior to 1965, US laws limited immigration by enforcing small quotas based on nation of origin. But the passage of the Hart-Celler Act expanded entry quotas and allowed easier entry for family members of US citizens and permanent residents. Equally important, Hart-Celler allowed for consideration of special skills.

The politics of the time, in part, drove this open door policy. The previous limitations on Asian immigrants resulted largely from the Immigration Act of 1924, aka the Johnson–Reed Act. The law included several pieces of explicit nativist legislation, including the National Origins Act and the Asian Exclusion Act. They were two pieces in a long line of discriminatory legislation aimed at preventing the increase of the Asian population in the United States. The Johnson-Reed Act capped the number of immigrants admitted from any country to 2% of the population of people from that country who were already living in the United States in 1890. (The Johnson-Reed Act was also designed to choke off immigration from Southern and Eastern Europe and the Middle East.)

That xenophobia began to give way in Washington, DC, when President John F. Kennedy, an American whose ancestors emigrated from Ireland, called the racist laws "nearly intolerable." As America convulsed with the civil rights movement, the hypocrisy of the legacy immigration laws became more evident and uncomfortable for politicians. After Kennedy's assassination, President Lyndon B. Johnson picked up the torch and worked with Senator Edward M. Kennedy to push through Hart-Celler.

An unintended but happy consequence of the new law was to allow the United States to rapidly scale up its science and engineering workforce as the space race and arms race was intensifying among the world's superpowers. Effectively, Hart-Celler opened the floodgates. The old immigration law allowed most Asian countries, such as Taiwan, only 100 immigrant visas per year. In 1965, the last year before Hart-Celler took effect, 47 Taiwanese scientists and engineers immigrated to the United States. In 1967, 1,321 immigrated to the United States, an increase of more than 2,500%.[19]

The majority of the newly arrived skilled immigrants had come from the developing economies of Asia. Not surprisingly, many chose to settle in California, where an explosive growth in technology industries (aerospace in Southern California and information technology in the Bay Area) was fueling robust econo-mies and immigrant communities from Asia, providing cultural touchstones for the new arrivals. By 1990, one-quarter of the engineers and scientists employed in California's technology industries were foreign-born—more than twice that of other highly industrialized states such as Massachusetts and Texas. Then the Immigration and Nationality Act of 1990 nearly tripled the number of immigrant visas awarded for special occupational talents, from 54,000 to 140,000.[20]

In Silicon Valley, the presence of these ambitious, hard-working immigrants quickly became a poorly kept secret. Valley insiders joked that IC engineers—meaning "Indian and Chinese" rather than "integrated circuit" (which is commonly abbreviated as IC)—built the region's tech industry. Silicon Valley legend and former Stanford engineering professor James Clark (who co-founded Netscape and later WebMD) famously sung the praises of Indian engineers in the pop-culture version of Silicon Valley history and the Internet in Michael Lewis's book *The New New Thing*.

Few doubted that these immigrant engineers had become significant contributors to the rapid growth and cycle of innovation of Silicon Valley. But how much of a contribution had they made?

Using a combination of US Census data and interviews with 175 immigrant entrepreneurs, AnnaLee Saxenian arrived at some surprising conclusions in the report "Silicon Valley's New Immigrant Entrepreneurs," published in 1999. Over a mere two decades, immigrant entrepreneurs in general, and Chinese and Indian entrepreneurs in particular, became a powerful force in Silicon Valley value creation and company formation. She found that Chinese or Indian engineers served as CEOs or leaders at roughly one-quarter of all high-technology businesses in Silicon Valley. The companies they ran accounted for 58,000 (mostly high-paying) jobs and more than $16.8 billion in sales. The swift rise of this cadre from 1980 to 1998 was breathtaking. Indian and Chinese CEOs managed 13% of Silicon Valley tech companies started between 1980 and 1984. That rose to 29% of Valley tech companies started between 1995 and 1998.

As I mentioned in the introduction, I stumbled upon Saxenian's research in 2006 when I was starting my own research on globalization at Duke University. Intrigued, I contacted her to ask if she was interested in updating the project with more current information about Silicon Valley immigrant entrepreneurs, and she agreed. I also proposed that we expand the survey to cover the entire nation to better determine the impact of immigrant entrepreneurs on the national economy. We decided to expand the project to include all immigrant entrepreneurs in defined high-technology fields.

The responses we obtained from 2,054 companies showed an even greater impact in Silicon Valley than Saxenian's previous research. We focused on companies that had significant revenues ($1 million or more) and had employees. The findings from our 2007 report, "America's New Immigrant Entrepreneurs," showed a rapid rise in the number of immigrant entrepreneurs even over the previous decade.[21] In our survey, more than half (52.4%) of Silicon Valley startups had one or more immigrants as a key founder, compared with the California average of 38.8%. A comparison with Saxenian's 1999 findings showed that the percentage of firms with Indian or Chinese founders had increased from 24% to 28%—despite the overall pie getting bigger, with there being far more tech startups. Indian immigrants outpaced their Chinese counterparts as founders of engineering and technology companies in Silicon Valley. Saxenian reported that 17% of Silicon Valley startups from 1980 to 1998 had a Chinese founder and 7% had an Indian founder. We found that from 1995 to 2005, Indians were key founders of 13.4% of all Silicon Valley startups, and immigrants from China and Taiwan were key founders in 12.8%.

The outsized impact of Indian founders was logical. Between 1990 and 2000, the population of Indian scientists and engineers (S&E) in Silicon Valley grew by 646% (while the total foreign-born S&E workforce grew by 246% and the region's total population of S&E, both native and foreign-born, grew by only 103%). The overall percentage of immigrant-founded companies in Silicon Valley almost perfectly matched the population at large. In Silicon Valley, 52% of the S&E workforce was foreign-born.

Our research reported in "America's New Immigrant Entrepreneurs" also showed that immigrant entrepreneurs—and their impact—in high-growth fields has spread well beyond Silicon Valley. Nationwide 25.3% of all engineering and technology companies established in the United States between 1995 and 2005 had at least one immigrant founder. The pool of immigrant-founded companies nationwide generated more than $52 billion in sales in 2005. This group of companies had created roughly 450,000 jobs. Of the national cohort, Indians constituted 26% of company founders. Immigrants from the United Kingdom, China, and Taiwan contributed to 7.1%, 6.9%, and 5.8% of all immigrant-founded businesses, respectively.

This research showed quite conclusively that immigrants were driving growth in the engineering and technology sectors far out of proportion to their representation in the population. It also validated my beliefs, gleaned from thousands of interactions with people in the field. Even as I tabulated these results, though, I was getting feedback that US immigration policy was chasing away potential startups.

The Immigrant Entrepreneur Tide Peaks

At every event I attended, another would-be entrepreneur told me a story of how he or she wanted to stay but couldn't due to visa problems. My inbox overflowed with accounts of visa hell. In May 2012, I updated the research that Saxenian and I had done in 2005 tracking immigrant founders of technology and engineering companies. My motive was to see if, in fact, the Immigrant Exodus had played out in Silicon Valley and across the country. Sadly, my fears were confirmed: in our follow-up, of the 2,042 companies we surveyed nationwide, the proportion of immigrant-founded companies had slid from 25.3% to 24.3%. This is within the statistical margin of error, but it does indicate one thing clearly: the rapid growth in immigrant entrepreneurship is stagnating, if not declining. Among 335 Silicon Valley technology and engineering companies, we found the numbers had dropped from 52.4% to 43.9%. This shows a significant slide in immigrant entrepreneurship in the most important region in the world for technology company formation.

The slide was less pronounced among Indian immigrant entrepreneurs. In our survey, 33.2% of immigrant company founders were Indian. But considering the huge volume of Indian H-1B entrants between 12 and 15 years ago and the clearly demonstrated higher propensity of Indian nationals to launch startups, we would have expected the number of Indian company founders to triple or quadruple. That did not happen. So, for some reason, those Indians who statistically should have been founding companies have chosen not to hang out their own shingle.

The implications of these findings are devastating. The juggernaut of immigrant entrepreneurship in tech and engineering companies has reversed course. The United States risks losing a key growth engine right at the moment when its economy is stuck in a deep ditch, growing slowly and struggling to create jobs. Silicon Valley is the leading indicator of national technology trends. What happens in Silicon Valley will likely spread to the rest of the country. Driven to despair, skilled immigrants have soured on America. As you will see in the next two chapters, the twin culprits of this decline are: improved economic and business prospects in other parts of the world, where fast-growing economies are creating significant entrepreneurial opportunities and career advancement, and a backward, destructive immigration policy.

CHAPTER 3

The Innovator's Dilemma: Leaving America for Greener Pastures

Genomics expert Jason Gang Jin, who I mentioned in the introduction, received his PhD from the University of California, San Diego, and went on to become the director of the Functional Genomics Lab at the prestigious Salk Institute. He specialized in a cutting-edge DNA chip analysis that applies principles of semiconductor chip technologies to create DNA microarrays as a high throughput for genomics studies. These arrays assist gene researchers by quickly scanning for the presence of gene expression at whole genome-wide level in a biological sample.

A Chinese expatriate, Jin maintained strong contacts in his home country and its scientific establishment. In 2000, Jin was invited by top universities and life sciences institutes in China to give lectures in this field. He realized it was necessary to establish a national core center of genomics and biochip technologies to support the R&D projects for academic labs and the biotech/pharmaceutical industry in China, as well as collaborative research and clinical studies from international academic institutes and biotech/pharmaceutical companies to be implemented in China. Jin proposed to build such a center, and his proposal was quickly approved.

In 2001, with a huge government grant and seed funding from life sciences shareholders, Jin and 10 top life sciences shareholders launched Shanghai Biochip in China. They launched a related company, ShanghaiBio, in the United States in 2005. The companies provide integrated genomic services and collaborative support for tissue-banking, microarrays, sequencing, and biomarker assays to Chinese and international life sciences researchers in academic institutes and biotech/ pharmaceutical companies for their discovery, translational, and clinical studies. The two entities also develop their own molecular diagnostics methods and products, and have collectively become one of the leading centers for gene-based translational research and companion diagnostics in China.

While Jin had a rewarding position in the United States and received a high salary, he saw the promise of China as a center for biotech research. Aside from the subsidies and the seed fund, the Chinese government was building out world-class laboratories and beefing up academic programs to feed a biotech ecosystem with local talent. In Jin's mind, the microarray field and genomics in general provided growth opportunities, but they would also serve as rich resources of translational and clinical research, tissue banking, and other activities conducive to drug and diagnostics product development that were costly and risky in the United States.

For the past decade, Jin has straddled the United States and China, working in both places to run these two companies to build high-quality technology and management platforms to support global business. The tight partnering between Shanghai Biochip and ShanghaiBio has grown to employ hundreds of technicians and scientists, mainly at R&D labs in Shanghai. ShanghaiBio does have a strong business development team and a wet R&D lab presence in the United States, but most of the technical and research work is performed back in China. Jin also lectures at a number of leading Chinese universities and life sciences conferences, providing valuable intellectual capital to Chinese scholars who, until recently, had to travel to the United

States to study with professors of that caliber. Jin has recruited other expat Chinese scientists to return to their country of birth and work as researchers and scientists.

Beyond Sand Hill Road

Immigrant entrepreneurs now have many options besides the United States. For the report "America's Loss Is the World's Gain," which was published by Kauffman Foundation in 2008, my research team surveyed 1,203 Indian and Chinese immigrants who had worked in or been educated in the United States and later returned to their home countries.[22] Our inquiries found that while immigration policies had caused some returnees to depart, the most significant factors in their decision to return home were career opportunities, family ties, and quality of life. A majority of this group also planned to launch businesses within a year.

Two years later we ran a follow-up survey on a more select group of entrepreneurs who had studied in the United States for at least a year and later returned to their home country to open a business. We wanted only entrepreneurs who had been operating their businesses in India or China for a year or longer, in order to provide a temporal perspective. The cohort was comprised only partially of high-tech entrepreneurs (56% of Indians, 33% of Chinese), but we felt it was representative of the types of risk-taking, high-talent immigrants who would typically start businesses in the United States as well.

The results were instructive, detailed in our report "The Grass Is Indeed Greener in India and China for Returnee Entrepreneurs." More than 60% of Indian and 90% of Chinese respondents said the availability of economic opportunities in their countries was a very important factor in the decision to return home. Furthermore, 72% of Indian and 81% of Chinese returnees said that the opportunities to start their own businesses were "better" or "much better" in their home countries. Only 14% of Indians and 5% of Chinese said that opportunities had been better in the United States. Speed of professional growth was also better back home for the majority of Indians (54%) and Chinese (68%).[23]

We also looked earlier into the career cycle of skilled immigrants to learn if perceptions and intentions were changing. In March 2009, Kauffman published, "Losing the World's Best and Brightest," in which we had analyzed the responses of 1,224 foreign nationals who were studying in institutions of higher learning in the United States or who had graduated by the end of the 2008 academic school year. The survey respondents comprised 229 students from China (and Hong Kong), 117 students from Western Europe, and 878 students from India.[24]

Of the respondents, very few indicated a desire to remain in the United States permanently—only 6% of Indian, 10% of Chinese, and 15% of European students. Many students wanted to stay for a few years after graduation if given a choice. But the largest group of respondents wanted to return home within five years—55% of Indian, 40% of Chinese, and 30% of European students.

The survey also found a highly mixed view of which country will provide the best job opportunities. Of Chinese respondents, 52% perceived their home country as having the best job opportunities; of Europeans respondents, 26% perceived their home country as having the best; and of Indians, 32% perceived their home country as having the best. This is hardly conclusive, but it shows a key shift. There is no longer a clear consensus that the United States provides better job opportunities.

Other research corroborates our findings. Researchers from Rutgers University, Penn State University, and the Tata Institute of

Social Sciences surveyed nearly 1,000 Indians who are currently undertaking, or have completed, graduate studies in the United States. From the sample group, "only 8% strongly preferred to remain in the US, with the remainder either planning to return to India (preferably after some work experience abroad) or feeling undecided about their future."[25]

Prominent academic leaders have also noted the changes and the problems. Tom Katsouleas, dean of the Pratt School of Engineering at Duke University, and my mentor, says, "It breaks my heart when some of our brightest students—who graduated from the top of their classes in countries like India and China—are forced to leave because of visa issues and when they can't start their own companies." He says he has noticed a distinct shift over the past decade in what students say about their opportunities. "Before most considered the United States their only option—now they believe they have good opportunities back home," he says.

Yannis C. Yortsos, dean of the Viterbi School of Engineering at the University of Southern California, says that most of the school's foreign students express a strong desire to stay in the United States for at least a few years after graduation. This is their first preference. Those who get jobs or go on to complete higher education certainly do, he says. However, "we have noted a trend for some Chinese students, particularly those from large cities, to return home as soon as they have good job opportunities at home; similarly, students from India are also increasingly returning home after they have some work experience, particularly if the conditions are right for them to return," he says.

Not all researchers agree this is the case. One study by the Oak Ridge Institute for Science and Education (ORISE) concluded that the five-year stay rates of foreign PhD students in the United States in 2009 had not dramatically decreased and has, in some cases, increased.[26] The cohort of PhD students they researched had come to the United States in 1997 or earlier (it usually takes about seven years to complete a PhD, and the report analyzed five-year stay rates). A subsequent analysis of the same ORISE data that was completed by the National Foundation for American Policy (NFAP) found that the five-year stay rates for Indian nationals who received PhDs in science and engineering had actually dropped 10 percentage points from 2000 to 2004.[27] The stay rates for the Chinese dropped by 6% in the same period.

Students from Asia occupy a high percentage of slots in the US STEM (Science, Technology, Engineering, and Mathematics) graduate degree programs. According to the National Science Foundation, "From 1989 to 2009, students from four Asian countries/economies (China, India, South Korea, and Taiwan) earned more than half of US science and engineering doctoral degrees awarded to foreign students (122,200 of 223,200)— almost 4 times more than students from Europe (30,000)."[28] The majority of all STEM graduates from US master's and doctoral programs choose to remain in the United States for one to three years after graduation during the legally permitted Optional Practical Training (OPT) period. But an increasing number are heading home, sheepskin in hand, learned in the ways of American innovation.

Huiyao Wang, who is director general of the Center for China and Globalization and vice chairman of the China Western Returned Scholars Association, has been researching the trend. He says that he has observed dramatic increases over the past decade in the numbers of entrepreneurs returning home. Data from the Chinese government and other sources he analyzed showed that while increasing numbers of Chinese students are going abroad, a far greater proportion of them are returning. He says that 330,000 students left China in 2011, of whom 160,000 came to the United States. The numbers of graduates returning increased from 50,000 in 2008 to 100,000 in 2009, to 130,000 in 2010, and to 180,000 in 2011.Wang says that many of these students are starting companies and helping China become more competitive.

Unfortunately, it's no longer a given that foreign students will flock to US universities for science and technology graduate studies. Countries competing for global talent have mounted strong campaigns to bring in skilled immigrant students. For example, in Canada, foreign science and engineering students comprised roughly 7% of undergraduate and 22% of graduate science and engineering enrollment in 2008. This represents a significant uptick from 4% and 14% in 1999.[29] In the United Kingdom, foreign students studying science and engineering rose from 32% of the total in 1999 to 47% in 1998. Nearly 60% of graduate students in mathematics, computer sciences, and engineering are foreign students, with the majority of this increase coming from students from China and India.[30] As the US experience illustrates, it is far easier to create a thriving technology ecosystem when high numbers of talented foreigners come to a country to study and put down roots while agglomerating local connections and professional ties.

Taken as a whole, research and the most recent statistics indicate that we are on the cusp of a rapid exodus of entrepreneurial and scientific talent. New research shows that the decline of immigrant entrepreneurship in high-growth fields has already occurred.

The Decline of Silicon Valley Entrepreneurship: Why the IIT Grads Are Going Home

The Indian Institutes of Technology (IITs) are India's most prestigious universities. Not long ago, Silicon Valley was the prime destination for graduates of IIT schools. My writing collaborator, Alex Salkever, actually covered this topic in detail in an award-winning article on Salon.com, "Technical Sutra," more than a decade ago.[31] These graduates could often land jobs at highly profitable, fast-growing companies in Silicon Valley.

But fewer and fewer IITians are coming to the United States now. Consulting firm Evalueserve surveyed 677 IITians in 2008 to find out what percentage stayed in India and what percentage went abroad. The results showed a clear trend.[32] From 1964 to 2001, 35% of IIT graduates went abroad. But only 16% left in 2002 and only 6% left in 2006. Broken down by country, 30% of IITians who graduated from 1964 to 2001 moved to the United States. That number declined to 9% from 2002 through 2008.

True, the IIT group tended to have a more favorable view of opportunities in India, most likely because they were the cream of the crop and enjoyed unique possibilities. And perhaps this colored their view of life in the United States. Before 2002, 13% of IIT graduates thought the United States offered a better standard of living. The percentage dropped to almost zero for respondents from 2002 through 2008. The report's authors noted, "The point of 'inflexion' with respect to this change seems to have occurred with the graduating class of 2002 and likely correlates to the growth of India's economy, which (since 2002) has recently been 8% to 9% per year in real terms and 14% to 15% in nominal terms." The continued slow growth of the US economy means that in all likelihood even fewer IITians will make the move.

While the flow of migrants is surely impacted by the faster growth and correspondingly better opportunities in India, I believe other related factors strongly influenced this shift in opinion and reduction in departures to the United States. Highly respected tech companies like Amazon.com, Google, and

Microsoft launched and grew Indian-based operations. Indian engineers can now work for world-class companies without leaving home. Bangalore has become a substitute for the Bay Area or Boston. At the same time, the rapid maturation of economies throughout the developing world means that technology businesses are now viable there. In fact, the developing world was attractive precisely because it suffered a brain drain for so many years. There was a total dearth of competition for many fast-growing niches in e-commerce, mobile, and social media, among other sectors. This lack of competition translates into better chances for these IITians to build the next Amazon at home rather than competing not only against Amazon but against a dozen other well-funded startups trying to do the same thing in the United States.

That, in part, is why Punit Gupta went home. Gupta graduated from the Indian Institute of Technology Guwahati in 2002. He worked in Switzerland for a year with MIRALab before pursuing further studies. He enrolled in a master's program in the highly regarded computer science department at the Georgia Institute of Technology. In 2005 Gupta decided to stop studying and start earning. He joined the core team of a service-based startup called Endeavor Telecom. After spending six years at the company, he wanted to launch his own enterprise. Doing so meant turning his back on one of the hottest employment markets in the history of the technology industry. IIT grads regularly got starting salaries of $180,000 from Silicon Valley tech giants.

Gupta wanted to return to his native India to launch PriceCheckIndia, a shopping and price comparison service targeting the fast-growing middle- and upper-class market in the subcontinent. Such a service in the United States would have met a market crowded with competitors. In the subcontinent, however, Gupta's company is breaking new ground. In India online services remain relatively immature in comparison to the saturated US market. And Gupta is glad to be home, in the country he loves, among childhood friends and family.

He is not alone in this choice. Sachin Bansal, 26, and Binny Bansal, 25, graduated with degrees in computer science from the Indian Institute of Technology Delhi in 2005. Sachin worked at Techspan for six months and then at Amazon India for a year and a half. Binny worked at Sarnoff India for a year and a half and then at Amazon India for eight months. In September 2007 they launched Flipkart. Their basic idea was to build an e-commerce company as good as Amazon.com but focused on the Indian market. Naturally they started with an online bookstore. Today they move everything from consumer electronics and kitchen gear to beauty items. The company has become the most successful Internet company in India. With more than $100 million in revenues, it is on track to hit $1 billion in revenue by 2015. Of course, launching an Amazon competitor in the United States would be far more difficult.

The upshot of all this? While many IIT students still seek out work in the United States, increasingly they prefer to stay home and see bigger opportunities in India. Like Gupta and the Bansals, they are choosing to roll the dice and start a company in India. As I have stated before, driving this decision has been the twin culprits of better economic prospects abroad and restrictive US immigration policies. For people like Gupta and the Bansals, the immigration strictures came largely due to the structure of the most commonly used visa for foreign workers in skilled professions, the well-known but poorly regarded H-1B.

CHAPTER 4

H-1B Visas and Immigration Limbo

Hardik Desai came to the United States in 2007 to get an MBA from the Fisher College of Business at Ohio State University (OSU). He took a venture capital class in the spring of 2008 and became excited by the world of venture capitalists and entrepreneurs. As part of a class project, Desai and two classmates built a business plan for a novel technology invented at OSU.

The technology is a way to diagnose a group of diseases—including painful bladder syndrome and irritable bowel syndrome—that currently do not have a single-step diagnostic method. Often patients endure pain and misdiagnosis for years before a proper diagnosis is made. Desai and his team named the venture IR Diagnostyx and prepared a detailed business plan around the technology. The plan won third place in an OSU competition. "We got enough positive feedback to realize that we wanted to launch the company once we graduated," said Desai.

Unfortunately, the third person on the team, who was a US citizen, had to bow out of the venture. This left two international students, both on OPT visas, to launch the company. Against great odds, Desai and his partner raised $300,000 in seed capital and hired a CEO. The company could then hire Desai, who began the process of applying for H-1B visas. The USCIS rejected his petitions and additional filings for an H-1B several times with no explanation.

Desai struggled to keep his startup dream alive, even during this critical period of company formation. During that difficult time, Desai mused, "With no end in sight with the visa issues, I don't know what should I be doing. Should I forget everything here and go back to India? My parents think I should, given how unkind and sad the whole visa process has been for me. Should I leave the company and look for a job? I just don't know what is the right answer." US immigration laws required that his company show proof of its ability to pay his salary for an extended period of time—something that is impossible for nearly all startups. Desai was forced to close the company, leaving the promising technology on the shelf. He later got his H-1B after he took a job with a Cleveland, Ohio, venture capital firm.

How the H-1B Harms the US Economy and Sours Immigrants on America

The story of Hardik Desai is a textbook example of why we are seeing a decline in the percentage of immigrant founders at Silicon Valley companies. His tale represents only one of the many ways that the current governance structure for H-1B visas damages entrepreneurship and harms both immigrant entrepreneurs and America.

For those unfamiliar with immigration law, a quick explanation of the H-1B is in order. I asked two attorneys—Cyrus D. Mehta, a New York immigration attorney and adjunct professor at Brooklyn Law School, and Charles H. Kuck, an Atlanta-based attorney who is a former president of the American Immigration Lawyers Association—to help me piece parts of this chapter together.

The H-1B is the primary work visa awarding entry into the United States for professionals with bachelor's degrees. Unlike student or visitor visas, the H-1B does allow a path to permanent residency if the employer sponsors the worker. The path is by no means guaranteed. That said, many H-1B holders enter the process with the specific intent of obtaining a green card for permanent residency as soon as possible.

The overwhelming majority of H-1B visas are issued to foreign workers in STEM fields, such as information technology, life sciences, and materials sciences. These are typically engineers, scientists, doctors, nurses, professors, and researchers.

If a foreign worker with H-1B status resigns or is fired from the sponsoring company, the worker needs to find another employer or leave the United States immediately. There is no grace period. If an H-1B holder wants to switch jobs, then the new employer must file for an H-1B visa even before he or she leaves the previous job.

On August 2, 2011, the Department of Homeland Security announced a policy that allowed entrepreneurs to be sponsored through their own companies, but the company must have an independent board of directors that can control their employment and continue to show that the company can support their ability to work in a professional capacity as required under the H-1B law, which could also include the company's ability to pay the going wage on a regular basis. While this presents a theoretical option, entrepreneurs say that it is extremely difficult to surmount the hurdles that the H-1B process creates.

Competition for H-1B visas is fast and furious. In 2012, the entire allotment of H-1B visas was filled within 10 weeks after the filing period began in April. "This is reminiscent of the H-1B usage prior to the recession, when in 2008 all of the H-1B allotment was used by April 2," Kuck said.

The restrictions on H-1B visa holders have a number of deleterious effects. Once H-1Bs have started the process of filing for a green card, they cannot change employers or or even take a new job with their current employer without getting pushed to the back of the queue. Visa holders are therefore shackled to their sponsoring employer while their careers stagnate, and they accept salaries that may be lower than they could otherwise make. By making it extremely difficult for these workers to launch their own companies, the law snuffs out the entrepreneurial ambitions of H-1B holders and encourages them to leave the United States to start a company elsewhere. That may, as is the case with Desai and IR Diagnostyx, limit the ability of immigrant founders to turn university-born technologies into viable products and companies. These types of university technologies constitute a massive untapped resource of intellectual firepower. Outside of a select group of top universities (Stanford, the Massachusetts Institute of Technology, California Institute of Technology) very few of the tens of thousands of inventions filed with university technology licensing offices ever turn into companies or even market review exercises.

The History of the H-1B Visa

The H-1B program was created in 1965 under the Hart-Celler Act as a means to allow US employers to temporarily hire foreign workers with specialty skills. It was modified in 1990 to add an annual cap and a labor attestation requirement. This requirement mandates the employer to pay either the prevailing or the actual wage for a given skill set (whichever is higher). The prevailing wage is determined by the US Department of Labor.

The stated term of the H-1B is three years with the option of extension for another three years. So, the maximum term is six years, but if the worker has filed for a green card before the sixth year and certain conditions are met, then the H-1B can be extended either one year or three years at a time until the green card is granted. In practice, many workers who enter on H-1B visas spend more than a decade waiting for permanent resident status. H-1B workers who are born in India and China face the longest queues in the green card backlogs, and many have to wait for a decade or longer before they can get a green card. H-1B workers who are not born in India and China, and who are sponsored under a green card category applicable to advanced degrees, do not have to wait for nearly as long. However, workers who were not born in India or China, if they are sponsored in another green card category applicable to positions requiring bachelor degrees or two years of experience, still have to wait at least five years.

In 1991, more than 50,000 H-1B visas were issued. The numbers rose steadily over the next two decades. This included significant increases during the run-up to the Y2K as the United States sought to prepare for what was then believed to be a major IT crisis that could significantly disrupt economic activity and open security breaches in networked IT infrastructures. In 1999, the number of H-1Bs issued exceeded 100,000. From 2001 to 2003, there were 195,000 visas issued. The US government dropped the cap on H-1B visas to 65,000 for fiscal year 2004, decreasing the supply. At present, the H-1B is capped at 65,000 visas for for-profit employers. An additional 20,000 visas are available for foreign students completing advanced degrees in the United States.

In most years, demand for these visas has vastly exceeded supply—except for 2001, when the cap was doubled. In that year, according to the Brookings Institution,[33] 287,519 applications for H-1B visas were made by employers, and 161,643 H-1B visas were issued. In 2008, when the cap was 65,000, there were 404,907 applications filed for H-1B visas, with 129,464 visas issued—that's less than one out of three. Institutions of higher education are exempt from the annual cap. Thus, when the numbers run out, only universities and nonprofits affiliated with universities can continue to employ foreign workers in order to remain globally competitive. Moreover, once a worker is counted under the cap from a prior year, a new H-1B filed by another employer is not counted again. Still, there is reluctance for H-1B workers to leave employers once the green card process has been started on their behalf.

Brookings also determined that H-1Bs are concentrated in metropolitan areas that tend to have dense research and technology clusters, such as Silicon Valley and New York City. These happen to be the places with the lowest unemployment rates for bachelor's degree holders. Even smaller cities with research centers have much higher concentrations of H-1B applications. Places such as Columbus, Indiana, where engine manufacturer Cummins is based, and Rochester, Minnesota, home of the medical giant Mayo Clinic, are among the regions with the highest demand for H-1Bs and the lowest unemployment rates for bachelor's degree holders. In other words, where there is innovation and economic growth, there is a great demand for US and foreign workers.

The Program Nobody Likes: Death Threats and H-1Bs

In September 2010, I gave the lunchtime keynote at an Immigra-tionWorks conference in Seattle, Washington. Immigration-Works is a pro-immigration advocacy and research group. I have participated in several immigration conferences, but this was not a normal keynote or conference. The speakers for this event received letters telling them that if they attended "the biggest gathering of traitors of the century ... they would do this at their own peril." Attached to the letters were M1 bullets (a carbine used in semiautomatic weapons by government and paramilitary forces). Security at the event included Federal

Bureau of Investigation agents, Seattle plainsclothes police, and a big bouncer at the door. The FBI agents asked me not to mention the threats until after the conference. Several of the invited speakers, including a senator, chose not to attend as a result of the threat.

Over the years, I have grown accustomed to being a target and a virtual punching bag for a vocal community that despises immigrant labor in skilled professions. Needless to say, the H-1B program is extremely controversial. Economists, politicians, and advocates for the employee rights of US-born technology workers have claimed that these types of visas are used as another form of outsourcing by Indian and US technology companies. Those companies, critics claim, use H-1Bs to import cheaper labor. Claims of a shortage of US STEM employees are exaggerated, say the H-1B opponents, who cite slow salary increases among STEM workers as evidence that the market is saturated with candidates. In fact, these critics blame the H-1Bs for depressed wages for US-born workers in technical fields.

To bolster their argument, they point to research done by labor economist George Borjas, who has reported that foreign workers in STEM fields "crowd out" native-born workers and depress salaries.[34] Academic and H-1B critic Norman S. Matloff believes that the H-1B allows companies to hire technical talent in hot programming fields or sectors but avoid market premiums.[35] The job classification system and salary index companies sponsoring for H-1Bs are required to only report broad sector averages and not subspecialty salary trends, Matloff said. This allows those companies to legally pay submarket wages by basing salaries to H-1Bs on broad indexes, which don't reflect reality.

It's easy to understand these concerns. Flouting employment discrimination laws, unethical body shops blatantly advertise in US publications for jobs that clearly target foreign nationals.

A search for visa-related terms such as *OPT, CPT,* and *F-1* on Dice.com, a leading technology recruiting site, turns up dozens of these listings. For example, an advertisement placed by AET Solutions, identified by a native workers' rights advocacy organization Bright Future Jobs in the report "No Americans Need Apply," has the title "Looking for fresh OPTs for training and placement in USA."[36] The Bright Future Jobs report correctly notes, "The ad only contains US Citizenship and Immigration Services (USCIS) abbreviations for visa workers but *not one* common Information Technology (IT) term. Americans about to graduate with the same technical degrees would likely never find this ad. Or, if they stumbled upon it, they would be confused."

Some government officials also feel that the H-1B program is abused as a means to provide cut-rate IT labor to US entities that set up the equivalent of onshore body shops. "Some of those applications are blatantly fraudulent or without merit—not even close, nothing that remotely looks like a real business case," one senior US consular employee, who is a friend and who asked to remain anonymous, told me. He said, "Those applications look more like vendors trying to cash in on demand for what is likely ordinary labor. This is not borderline abuse. It's flagrant."

These violations are real, but they comprise a minority percentage of H-1B applications. In September 2008, the USCIS stated in its H-1B Benefit Fraud & Compliance Assessment that 21% of H-1B visas received emerged from improper applications.[37] This included technical violations as well as clear fraud. (The USCIS has made concerted efforts to reduce fraud since then, but according to sources I have corresponded with inside the US consular system, H-1B fraud is still occurring.)

Numerous H-1B workers have also told me that they feel they are underpaid. While conclusive evidence of institutional underpayment has yet to emerge, the US Department of Justice has on two occasions mandated that groups of H-1B employees receive payments collectively totaling hundreds of millions of dollars to compensate for years of below-market wages. In a nutshell, both the H-1B holders and the advocacy groups championing native-born IT workers feel they are the victims—and there is some truth to both of their claims. Some of the recommendations I make in chapter 6 will address the fundamental problems with these visas.

Good for America, Good for Innovation

For their part, tech companies, venture capitalists, and entrepreneurs say that the shortage of technology workers is real and cannot be accounted for by merely tallying the numbers of native-born STEM degree holders in the United States. Skill requirements (programming languages, for example) shift rapidly, rendering skills of significant parts of the workforce obsolete and requiring significant upgrading. As someone who has run a startup, I have experienced this firsthand. When I was running Seer and Relativity, I wanted the best programmers I could find, and finding great Java programmers was very, very hard. That is why we ended up using a team in Russia for some of our software development. Many of these Russians immigrated to America—when it was relatively easy. They are now working for leading technology companies.

Another argument that H-1B liberalization advocates lay out, which I also agree with, is that many US STEM degree holders have long since left the field for other pursuits, such as finance and law—which sometimes pay higher wages. This has been particularly pronounced in the past decade as Wall Street salaries have soared and the big banks and hedge funds have aggressively recruited geeks to become data-driven analysts and write algorithms for black-box trading systems.

In a similar vein, H-1B opponents fail to take into account the lack of labor mobility in the United States. The country has the highest rate of home ownership in the world, something that tends to limit mobility. That mobility has been further diminished by the depressed home prices, which prevent technical workers who may be underwater on their mortgages from switching to other jobs. Another reason why American workers may be reluctant to go where the jobs are is because of the comparatively high cost of living in areas where tech job growth is highest, such as San Francisco and Silicon Valley. What's more, techies in other parts of the United States may have trouble keeping up with the latest in programming trends and developing job skills that will position them in the industry. Because few US companies are willing to retrain workers in new programming languages, this makes it hard for them to stay on the technology treadmill.

While critics of the H-1B system have claimed that recipients going into work at universities and research institutions tend to comprise lower-caliber candidates, the reality is that many of the country's most prestigious research institutions—the University of California system, the University of Michigan, the Ivy League, the National Institutes of Health—are strongly represented among the ranks of H-1B employers. These schools can take their pick of the crop—they don't have to compromise. Take the case of the Mayo Clinic in Rochester, Minnesota. That single institution, which primarily seeks worker status for life scientists and health practitioners, accounts for 71% of the metropolitan area's H-1B applications.[38]

A growing body of research, too, has found that a higher concentration of H-1B holders in STEM fields actually boost invention, a strong proxy for technology advancement. In their work "How Much Does Immigration Boost Innovation?" Jennifer Hunt and Marjolaine Gauthier-Loiselle found that each 1% increase in the population of immigrant college graduates increased overall patents per capita by 9% to 18%.[39] In another research paper, "The Supply Side of Innovation," William Kerr of Harvard Business School and William Lincoln of the University of Michigan studied the impact of the concentration of H-1B visa holders in given metro areas with regard to innovation.[40] Kerr and Lincoln reported a 10% increase in H-1B population corresponded with a 1–4% increase in Indian and Chinese invention (measured as patents).

To some degree, the H-1B dynamic is simply a numbers game. The STEM fields represent the fastest growing job categories. According to the National Science Foundation's Science and Engineering Indicators (2012), only 4% of the world's undergraduate engineering degrees go to US citizens. In contrast, 56% are earned in Asia, and 17% of engineering degrees are awarded to Europeans. Smaller Asian nations manage to exceed the United States in undergraduate engineering and science degrees; the combined natural sciences and engineering degrees awarded in South Korea, Taiwan, and Japan exceed the combined degree tally for the United States. Not surprisingly, more than two-thirds of all H-1B requests are issued for positions in the STEM fields, according to research at Brookings; likewise, more than two-thirds of those STEM-based H-1B visas go to applicants from India and China.[41]

In a global competition for talent, US companies and institutions say they must seek the best talent, whatever the nationality of the candidate. And that's only rational. The National Basketball Association looks all around the world for the best talent, and increasingly it has found the top players outside the United States, from Manu Ginobili to Yao Ming to Tony Parker to Pau Gasol. Asking US technology and engineering companies to restrict their search geographically makes as much sense as telling the NBA it can't recruit players from outside the United States. Such a mandate would reduce the level of talent in the league, just as placing tighter strictures on H-1Bs and green cards would further reduce the level of science and engineering talent in the United States.

To summarize, the advocates of a more open immigration policy feel the H-1B program limits the entry of global talent into the United States and should be significantly expanded. Detractors of the H-1B program feel it promotes wage arbitrage and a modern version of indentured servitude that depresses the wages of US workers in STEM fields. I agree with aspects of both arguments, but I believe that allowing for a more liberal H-1B policy will end any semblance of wage depression, as talented immigrants would quickly achieve market wages for their skills. Most important, the history of the world shows that open economies grow faster than closed ones. Labor represents one of the most critical economic inputs. Yet US policy still views the average H-1B immigrant as a number rather than as a contributor.

First-Class Minds, Second-Class Citizens

Puneet Arora arrived in the United States in 1996 for a residency in internal medicine at Southern Illinois University. He entered on a J-1 visa, designed for work-study exchange programs. He excelled and was accepted into advanced fellowship programs in endocrinology, first at New York University and then at the Mayo Clinic—two of the premier medical research institutions in the United States. Arora was allowed to remain in the United States by signing up to practice medicine in an underserved area, part of a push by the US federal government to recruit health-care professionals to work in locations lacking in doctors and nurses. During that period he spent five years teaching at the University of Minnesota School of Medicine and working in private practice, treating patients and giving back to America.

A temporary change in an immigration rule in 2007 allowed Arora and his wife to file for a change of status and receive an Employment Authorization Document. He was then able to begin work in the private sector in 2008 as a clinical director at Amgen, where he became a key contributor in early-stage drug development efforts for compounds targeting cardiovascular-metabolism and inflammation disorders tied to endocrinology. He went on to become the medical director at Genentech in October 2011.

Arora received numerous awards and his research won praise from his peers. He also gave back, teaching extensively and serving on numerous society boards and as a special judge at the 2011 Intel Science Fair. He clearly showed not only his exceptional scientific capabilities but also a willingness to be a good citizen and contributor to the United States. During all that time—his entire adult professional life—Arora did not know whether he would ever be able to attain permanent citizenship in the United States. In July 2012, after 16 years of living in immigration limbo, Arora finally received his green card. He is now considering the possibility of launching his own startup. But he cautions other doctors who might choose to come to the United States by the same pathway as he did. "It was a huge relief not to be applying for more renewals. I'm very glad to have finally received my green card and plan to stay here forever," Arora said. "But I would advise serious caution on coming here with a J-1 visa if the current policies don't change and the country caps and overall caps remain the same."

In every major US city, at every US university, in every major US technology company, in every hospital, you can find people like Puneet Arora—high achievers who have been stuck in limbo many years. The cause of this problem is simple. During the run-up to Y2K and the dot-com boom, the United States significantly boosted H-1B permits. Since then it has failed to boost the number of green cards available to those H-1B holders. This has led to an enormous bubble of smart, talented people like Arora.

How big is that bubble? More than one million people. We touched on this in our 2010 report titled "How Many Highly Skilled Foreign-Born Are Waiting in Line for US Legal Permanent Residence?" Working with my research team, New York University professor Guillermina Jasso estimated that as of September 30, 2006, there were 499,680 principals in the main employment-based categories and an additional 556,541 family members awaiting legal permanent resident status in the United States. The number of employment-based principals waiting for labor certification—the first step in the US immigration process—was estimated at 184,545 in 2006. The number of pending I-140 applications—the second step of the immigration process—stood at 50,132 in 2006. This was more than seven times the total in 1996 (6,743). The number of employment-based principals with approved I-140 applications and unfiled or pending I-485s—the last step in the immigration process—was estimated at 309,823 in 2006, representing almost a threefold increase from the previous decade.[42]

Overall, we estimated that the number of employment-based principals (in the three main employment visa categories— EB-1, EB-2, and EB-3) waiting for legal permanent residence in the United States in 2006 was 499,680. The total number of employment-based principals in the focal employment categories and their family members waiting for legal permanent residence in the United States in 2006 was estimated at 1,056,221. We further estimated that 126,793 residents abroad were also waiting for US legal permanent residence, giving a worldwide total of 1,183,014. That is nearly 1.2 million people stuck in immigration limbo.

According to information posted on the websites of the State Department and the USCIS, in the last five years visas in the EB-1 category—which is for priority workers, including geniuses—have continued to be available so that processing can begin immediately. In all of the employment categories, however, the problem of too few visas remains. For all applicants, there is a wait of several years. For Indians and Chinese, the waits are the longest.

The problem is twofold—the imbalance between the number of slots open in a given year and the number of applicants, and the applicant's nationality. The United States allots 140,000 green cards per year to employment-based (EB) visas. But there are far more applicants for these visas. Furthermore, the law stipulates that each nationality may receive no more than 7% of the total number of employment-based green cards. Considering that Indian and Chinese recipients make up more than 50% of the total H-1B holder pool, it's obvious that this represents a severe bottleneck.

This has fed the queue and created an entire underclass of H-1B holders who cannot leave the United States (they would lose their place in the queue, because their employers would withdraw their petitions), who struggle to switch jobs and ask for raises, and who cannot open their companies or employ themselves. For the spouses of H-1B holders, the situation is far grimmer. H-4 visa holders are not allowed to work at all. If they are caught working illegally, they are deported. In some states, it is impossible for H-4 visa holders to obtain a driver's license. As a result, hundreds of thousands of spouses who may have valuable skills in science or medicine are sitting on their hands, unable to contribute or work in the United States. And many of them, in states and regions where driving is the only way to get around, are literally trapped in their homes. This is hardly a situation you would expect to face in America.

Against this backdrop of growing green card queues and bureaucratic hurdles, and highly restrictive spousal employment rules for H-1Bs, the economies of India and China have clocked rapid growth. For Chinese or Indian students holding graduate degrees in STEM fields, the choice of pursuing an H-1B with an uncertain future or moving home to work at a university or for a large multinational, or to start their own company, is no longer as easy to make. This has been particularly true for the last five to seven years, as the US economy has stalled and shrunk.

Equally important, as I previously discussed, is to consider the average duration of time immigrant entrepreneurs spend in the United States before launching their own company: 13 years. This means large numbers of the cohort that entered the United States during the Y2K run-up—the largest H-1B cohort ever— are likely to be considering whether to start a business. From the research data I covered in chapter 2, we can conclude that at least some of them are deciding either not to start a business or, more likely, to start a business somewhere else. Right now we should see a spike in immigrant-founded tech startups as a result of the large spike in H-1B entrants we saw 15 years ago during the Y2K run-up.

On a personal note, if I were a young immigrant technologist in my mid-30s, stuck on an H-1B visa in America, and trapped in a middling job, I would probably have decided to return to Australia or India. What's more, Australia and a growing list of countries might have actually tried to recruit me as a skilled immigrant candidate. Those countries have recognized the success of Silicon Valley and the US technology sector, and they are making a concerted effort to attract skilled immigrants to build similar successes outside the United States.

CHAPTER 5

How the World Is Trying to Steal Silicon Valley's Thunder

On July 25, 2012, the founders of 52 new companies landed in Santiago, Chile, to pursue startup dreams. This group of founders had applied to Start-Up Chile, a two-year-old incubator and accelerator program funded by the Chilean government. The July arrivals completed the fourth class in the program, which accepts new entrants on a semiannual basis. More than 25 countries are represented in this round of Start-Up Chile participants, with founders hailing from Argentina, Canada, Chile, China, India, Spain, Sri Lanka, the United Kingdom, the United States, Uruguay, and Venezuela.

The goal of the program is to build a more diversified Chilean economy with a robust technology sector. Chile banked huge sums of cash during the natural resource booms of the past decade. It's copper mining, forestry, and fishing operations gave the country a surplus of many billions of dollars. But the Chilean government wanted to build an information technology sector that could compete in the global economy and give talented Chileans good jobs while boosting the national economy with companies not tied to boom-and-bust cycles of natural resources.

From what I can tell, they are well on their way to succeeding in this endeavor. Start-Up Chile has attracted a diverse set of entrepreneurs. Maptia, built by a team of geographers, economists, and coders who are British, Chinese, and Swiss, seeks to revolutionize online mapping technology to allow brands and individuals to capture untapped value inherent in geotagged visual content. Andean Designs, with the team hailing from India, seeks to create designer ceramics based on Andean culture. Biometry Cloud, with a team from Chile, is selling cloud-based pattern-recognition web services, APIs, and libraries for mobile devices. The company Dr. Busca, with a team from Brazil, allows patients to book doctor appointments online from mobile devices. Start-Up Chile has attracted a number of entrepreneurs from the United States, as well. H2020 uses mobile phones to collect and map water data to help communities and industries understand the dynamics of their water resources.

For me, the arrival of this class—the largest ever—provides both satisfaction and sadness. Back in 2010, Chile's minister of economy, Juan Andrés Fontaine, and his head of innovation, Nico Shea, asked me to help them crack the code for attracting high-value, high-growth companies. So I helped them create Start-Up Chile. The idea seemed a bit nutty to outsiders. Give $40,000 to startups led by foreign entrepreneurs to move and set up shop in one of the most magnificent places on this planet for six months—no strings attached. Yes, if the founders decided they wanted to leave at the six-month mark on the dot, the government would bid them farewell with no hard feelings. As part of the package, the Chilean government planned to help them settle in, provide free office space, teach them Spanish, and connect them to investors and mentors.

This was part of a crazy plan I helped the government of Chile implement. They wanted a startup scene. They had little. I told them to bet on smart people and creative entrepreneurs. Put as many of them in one place as possible and they would create a scene themselves, because like seeks out like, and the concepts of economies of scale and tipping points also apply to entrepreneurship. To attract these people, I told the Chilean government, make it as easy as possible to start a business. Give them enough money to live on. Give them a place to work. Give them easy immigration status. Don't place punitive penalties on them if their efforts don't work out and they need to start again.

This was a radical departure from common practices for building innovation hubs. To date, a government or an organization seeking to do this would construct a science park next to a research university or research institute and offer big tax breaks to targeted industries that set up shop there. The focus has always been on industry and real estate—not people. It is telling that not one of the hundreds of these top-down efforts anywhere in the world, including some in Chile, have delivered the hoped-for results. Silicon Valley is what everyone has tried to re-create, but this did not spring forth from tax breaks or targeted incentives to industry. Rather, Silicon Valley evolved because a critical mass of maverick thinkers and tinkerers came together from all over the world. It is this diversity and people-to-people Silicon Valley magic that Start-Up Chile has tried to create.

Thus far, Start-Up Chile has surpassed expectations. Our biggest concern was that few entrepreneurs, other than those from similar or even poorer Latin American countries, would agree to relocate their companies so distant from the existing nexuses of innovation to a remote place like Chile. To date, Start-Up Chile has received more than 1,600 applications from 70 countries, with the most coming from the United States. The startups in the program employ not only foreign entrepreneurs but also hundreds of locals. The early foreign startup participants pulled in $8 million in venture capital financing from venture capital funds in Argentina, Brazil, France, the United States, and Uruguay.

The program has sparked a spread of Silicon Valley–style entrepreneurship around Chile. There are now tribes of entrepreneurs and locals to build expertise on diverse topics, from biotech to consumer products to software-as-a-service to social media. The pairing of locals wanting to broaden their horizons with Start-Up Chile participants made such an impression that many of the Chileans I spoke to after the program started became interested in launching their own high-growth startups. In a nod to this development, the government of Chile opened the program to local entrepreneurs in July 2011. In short order they received a flood of 600 applications. Today, dozens of home-grown startups are participating in the program.

Start-Up Chile now has an annual budget of about $15 million, and its momentum is building. The success of this program has convinced me that I was right—the magic happens when you focus on feeding the dreams of people rather than putting up buildings. Through the Kauffman Foundation, which supports Start-Up Chile, representatives from dozens of nations around the globe have sought information and resources on how to launch similar programs in their own countries. On the one hand, I am very happy to see young entrepreneurs get a chance to build companies in such a supportive environment. On the other hand, I am sad that these companies did not or could not start up in the United States.

Santiago cannot compete with Silicon Valley yet. The program has had a number of high-profile startups decamp for Silicon Valley (such as Babelverse and CruiseWise). But few would argue that Chile could one day grow into a viable competitor to Silicon Valley. And only three years ago, Start-Up Chile was not even an idea. Despite its short tenure and the difficulty attracting global talent to a remote location with immature capital markets and a nonexistent startup ecosystem, the program has already eclipsed lesser US cities as a startup mecca in a mere two years. That is quite impressive.

The Race to Capture Entrepreneurial Talent and Skilled Immigrants

Chile's story is one of many examples of concerted efforts by governments to attract and retain talented immigrants. Australia, Canada, China, Germany, New Zealand, Singapore, and the United Kingdom have all put in place programs that offer a variety of enticements to highly skilled immigrants, ranging from expedited citizenship to tax credits to relocation assistance to legal help to gaining access to residence permits for restricted cities. Many of these measures are aimed directly at solving the problems that immigrants have long suffered in trying to stay in America for their careers or to launch companies. All of these countries share a willingness to put economic over political goals.

These solutions have not been perfect. Unemployment and underemployment rates among skilled Russian Jewish immigrants to Israel, for example, were initially quite high, despite the fact that the Israeli economy is heavily focused on the generation of companies in engineering, IT, and life sciences. (The rate lowered over time as the immigrants assimilated.) Whatever the case, taking a look at some of the strategies these countries pursued could give clues as to how to better attract skilled labor to the United States and reform US immigration policies. The Partnership for a New American Economy put together an exhaustive paper[43] on the topic outlining the key differences I discuss in this chapter; it is well worth reading, and I built my arguments in part on their findings.

Australia: The government of the country has not awarded subsidies or specific privileges for startups (which Chile has done), but rather has tried to make it easier for skilled immigrants in selected fields to attain permanent residency. In 2012, Australia raised the annual cap on permanent residency visas for skilled immigrants and their families to 126,000.[44] The United States issues 140,000 employment-based green cards each year for immigrants and their families. The US population is more than 10 times larger than that of Australia.[45] Obviously, Australia values employment immigration more highly on a per capita basis. Unlike the United States, Australia allows regional governments to award preference for specific skill sets and bring in skilled immigrants to meet regional needs. International students who are considered to be highly qualified can remain in the country working for 18 months after graduation. This is six months longer than the standard OPT tenure awarded to foreign students in the United States. Australia has announced the launch of an online process to screen applicants and allow those with the proper qualifications to apply for a visa. It is not uncommon for a skilled immigrant to receive notice of permanent residency before they even arrive in Australia.

Canada: The Canadian government assigns applicants number grades based on key factors such as age, education, and work experience. The Canadian immigration ministry can base immigration decisions on economic development goals without requiring legislative change, giving them unprecedented flexibility from year to year on targeting skill sets in immigrants. A foreign undergraduate or graduate degree holder can, upon getting a diploma, get a work permit for up to three years without having secured a job in advance. To retain students in STEM fields, Canada allows PhDs in those disciplines to apply for permanent residency while they are still enrolled in school. And like Germany and Chile, Canada offers visas to entrepreneurs with viable business plans even in the absence of funding.[46]

China: The Chinese government has a National Medium- and Long-Term Talent Development Plan designed to encourage successful Chinese-born expatriates to come home and work or start a business. The program is extraordinarily generous. The most accomplished returnees are eligible to receive low six-figure cash bonuses (in US dollars). Lower-level scientists with Western PhDs but little experience are eligible to receive a bonus in the high five figures. Expats who return can get housing subsidies or free housing in the Chinese city of their choosing. Returning entrepreneurs may also receive multiyear exemptions from business taxes.[47]

Germany: Historically a country closed to immigration, Germany had many guest workers but little immigration. To deal with growing labor shortages in the fast-growing STEM fields, Germany rolled out a special "green card" program that put in place a fast track for non-European IT experts that would allow them to live in Germany on a temporary basis.[48] Germany also allows senior academic researchers, top-level business managers, and others who are highly skilled to gain permanent residency very quickly. Like Chile, Germany has a visa program for startups that allows them to come and launch their companies legally in Germany without any funding. All that's required is a credible business plan.

Singapore: Skilled immigrants can apply for and quickly receive Employment Passes allowing them to work and later seek permanent residency. Unlike in the United States, the spouses of skilled immigrant workers in Singapore can legally work. Singapore's EntrePass program allows a foreign national with a business plan approved by the government and $50,000 from investors to build a business there for a year.[49] If their business is performing well, the government offers visa renewals. In select cases for particularly promising businesses, the government will match investments from the private sector.

It's evident that in designing their employment immigration policies, many countries have pointedly addressed some of the problems that skilled immigrants encounter in the US system. They have learned from the mistakes of the United States.

One country that is perhaps the biggest competitor to the United States for entrepreneurial talent but was not mentioned in this chapter is India. That is because India does not have a strategy to attract talented people—it does not need it. It offers an exploding market and a culture that its people want to return to.

The United States faces a far lower hurdle than any of the countries mentioned in this chapter. If the United States reformed its immigration policies and made it easier for startups and technology innovators to both move to the United States to launch companies and to remain as permanent residents, this would prove to be an irresistible magnet. The Immigrant Exodus would reverse course almost immediately, because what other countries are trying to build, the United States already has, in spades. The fixes I suggest in the next chapter to reverse this exodus may meet some political headwinds, but they are essential to ensuring that America maintains its position as the world's most important place for science, technology, and engineering innovation.

CHAPTER 6

Seven Fixes to Slow the Immigrant Exodus

Rudrava Roy is an Indian citizen and engineer. He lived in the United States from 2000 to 2011 and worked as a researcher at one of the leading universities. But he had to leave academia and get a full-time job because of visa issues. His friend's startup sponsored his H-1B visa, and he worked there for five years. During that time he built three products from scratch, one of which he holds a patent on. For the small company to apply for a green card for him, it would have had to spend more than $10,000 in legal fees and prove that Roy could be fully employed during the many-year wait, which it could not.

During the last two years of his six-year H-1B period, Roy also started consulting with a small manufacturing company in a niche market. He helped the company build a completely new product that was half the cost of both its existing offerings and its competitor's offerings. The product received an award at the Consumer Electronics Show in Las Vegas. The client was keen to take Roy on as a full-time employee but couldn't get an H-1B visa.

So Roy left the United States in the fall of 2011 and returned to India. The manufacturing company still needed his services, so it outsourced Roy's work to an Indian company, which in turn hired him. Had the immigration process presented less of an obstacle, the jobs that Roy created in India would likely never have left the United States.

In previous chapters I discussed how America is now tipping into an Immigrant Exodus and why this is happening. Cases like Roy's illustrate why something that should be quite simple—extending visas and permanent residency to highly skilled employees—has become extremely difficult. I covered the problems and perils of the current H-1B visa program and how the H-1B discourages immigrants from launching startups. Last, I showed how other countries are beefing up their programs to recruit talented immigrants who in decades past would have relocated to the United States without hesitation.

There are relatively simple fixes to all of these problems. These fixes will cost US taxpayers next to nothing. Collectively, these changes to immigration policy and law will drive significant economic growth for the US economy both in terms of innovations and companies founded. To be clear, the economies of countries like Brazil, China, and India will continue to grow, and these countries will offer stiff competition for the United States for talent. But rather than competing with one arm tied behind our backs, we will be competing from a position of strength. We will still lose some talent, but we will also gain talent that's eager to come to the United States.

1. Increase the number of green cards available to skilled immigrants.

If the United States was to increase by three or four times the number of employment-based green cards issued per annum and simultaneously eliminate the 7%-per-country limit that I discuss in number 7, the bottleneck for green cards would instantly disappear. The wait times for green cards would go back to what they used to be when Sophie Vandebroek and I each came to the United States. We would not be taking any American jobs away or creating any social problems with a large influx—these doctors, engineers, scientists, and teachers are already here working for American companies. They are just stranded in limbo, wasting the most productive parts of their lives worrying about whether they will be able to stay in the United States and contribute to its success. Hundreds of thousands of families would plant deep roots in US society. They would buy houses, become more active in their communities, and begin to dream the American Dream, just like previous generations of immigrants once did.

2. Allow spouses of H-1B visa holders to work.

Just as training top STEM students in US universities and then forcing them to leave is senseless, so too is preventing the spouses of H-1B holders from working and enjoying the same rights as anyone in the United States.

No research has yet been conducted on the composition of the H-1B spouse cohort in terms of educational and employment background (it would certainly be an interesting project). Anecdotally I hear that these spouses tend to be as skilled as their partners and often have STEM backgrounds.

Removing this major source of frustration and unhappiness for H-1B holders would certainly help slow the ongoing Immigrant Exodus.

3. Target immigration based on required skills.

In principle, the US workforce should be able to retrain quickly to meet skill needs in industries that are growing rapidly and require specific technical acumen. The reality is quite different. Demand for mobile phone developers (particularly for iPhone developers) has far outstripped supply, leading salaries to skyrocket and recruitment to bottleneck at companies seeking to build mobile apps, for example. The United States already practices some immigration targeting in life sciences professions for nurses or general practitioners and pediatricians, who are in short supply in many parts of the country. But a more developed program to bring in skilled immigrants for specific technical needs could accelerate economic development and business formation in the United States, in particular in fast-moving fields such as mobile development, big data analytics, and computational biology. These are, by the way, fields where foreign students in US universities already have a strong presence.

4. Untether the H-1B worker from the employer.

In the United States, H-1B holders cannot change jobs without getting government-sponsorship approval. This is a lengthy and risky bureaucratic process that often leads to rejection.

Making a change to allow the H-1B holder to work for any employer would have a number of positive impacts. First, it would allow talented H-1B holders to obtain salaries on par with their peers, eliminating wage compression for this group. Second, it would allow these workers to more easily switch their jobs and advance their careers in the United States while improving their skills and responding to market signals. This type of movement is essential for a broad, healthy labor market, and it is even more essential in areas such as IT where a relatively significant percentage of employees are H-1B holders. This would likely necessitate also allowing H-1B visa holders to pay for their own visa processing, an act that is currently prohibited. Currently, employers must pay all the costs for the H-1B visa filings.

5. Permanently extend the term of OPT for foreign students from one to four years.

As we read with the case of Hardik Desai, a single year of OPT is barely enough to get started on work and prove your mettle. In some cases, OPT can be extended to 29 months, as per changes initiated under the administration of President George W. Bush. But this covers only a restricted list of specialties and does not cover startup formation. I propose extending the work term for immigrant graduates of US universities and colleges to surpass Canada's term of three years. To be clear, I am against the idea of simply stapling a green card to the diploma of every STEM graduate. This practice would bring in the chaff with the wheat and could encourage the development of "green card diploma mills," where a student's primary purpose would be to obtain a green card. However, over the course of four years, a student on OPT should be able to either make significant headway in a startup business, significant progress in a career, or significant advancement in scientific research. Those who do well should be offered a path to a green card based on their merit.

6. Institute a startup visa.

This has been the number one demand from Silicon Valley and the venture capital community. The stories of immigrant entrepreneurs either suffering significant delays in getting work visas or having to leave the United States due to visa issues are now legion. The Startup Visa Act would provide a solution to this problem. In the US Congress, several members have proposed and are advocating the adoption of legislation to create a visa designed to aid foreign entrepreneurs. Representatives Carolyn Maloney (D-NY) and William L. Owens (D-NY) and Senators John Kerry (D-MA), Dick Lugar (R-IN), and Mark Udall (D-

CO) have all proposed legislation to establish an employment-based, conditional immigrant visa for a sponsored alien entrepreneur. These bills, introduced in 2010 and 2011, have died in committee.

The latest effort, in May 2012, is a bill introduced by Senators Jerry Moran (R-KS), Mark Warner (D-VA), Marco Rubio (R-FL), Roy Blunt (R-MO), Chris Coons (D-DE), and Scott Brown (R-MA). This bipartisan legislation was also introduced in the House by a large bipartisan group of representatives. The bill contains a wide variety of provisions designed to encourage immigrant entrepreneurship in America and to staunch the outflow of skilled STEM immigrants.

The Startup Visa legislation being proposed would provide foreign entrepreneurs with the ability to live in the United States and work for the companies that they start. To ensure that a business is legitimate, a startup would be required to raise a minimum level of financing from accredited investors. If after a certain number of years, the startup was employing a certain number of American workers, the entrepreneurs would qualify for green cards. We can debate the required investment levels and the number of jobs to be created, but a Startup Visa makes eminent sense. There is no downside for the United States.

There is a downside, however, for holders of this visa—if their venture fails or doesn't go anywhere, they must start again or leave the United States. But that's entrepreneurship—there are no guarantees. This won't appeal to everyone, and it is not meant to. The Startup Visa is for risk takers, and people who take risks form companies that create jobs. Right now, these job creators have no choice but to take their ideas and savings home with them and become our competitors. This legislation allows them to create the jobs in the United States.

7. Remove the country caps on green cards.

Because of the 7% per country limits, workers from high-population countries have to wait many times longer than workers from low-population countries to get permanent-resident visas. India gets the same quota as Iceland and China the same as Mongolia. This is what is contributing the most to the painful purgatory that immigrants from India and China face, and why their wait times stretch longer than a decade.

More than 35% of the world's population and an even higher percentage of the highly skilled global workforce lives in China and India. With a larger population comes more intense competition internally, so the quality of the skilled immigrants is even greater and the pool of applicants larger, and this presents more options for companies relying on innovation. So we are not only punishing the immigrants, but also our companies.

These caps need to be removed. Aman Kapoor, the co-founder of the immigration advocacy group Immigration Voice is spearheading efforts to put these changes into law. He says that removing per-country limits will create a "first come, first served" true merit-based system for equally qualified highly skilled immigrants. He says "such a change will benefit one and only one country in the world—the United States of America."

How Much Economic Value Could These Changes Drive?

This is the multi-billion-dollar question. My earlier research into the economic impact of immigrant founders in Silicon Valley and nationwide determined that the immigrant-founded startups in the technology and engineering sector alone employed 450,000 workers and generated $52 billion in revenue in 2005.[50] That is far more than the number of permanent residence visas we issued in the decade before this. Immigrants also coauthored 25% of the global patents, which give America a global advantage.

There is no reason that we couldn't double or triple the number of immigrant-founded startups and increase the amount of innovation we create. Even though the tide is turning, there are still millions of innovators all over the world who would come to the United States if we let them. So, within the next decade, these measures could conservatively add $100 billion to $150 billion in revenues to the US economy and generate between 1 million and 1.5 million jobs. The multiplier effects of the technology sector is among the highest of any economic sector, so revenues generated by this crop of startups would create many second- and third-order jobs outside of the sector or in related fields. Right now, there is simply no other segment of the US economy that could produce so much value and so many jobs so quickly. Again, these are conservative estimates. If the next Apple, Google, or Microsoft is among this crop of immigrant-founded startups, then the net new job and revenue generation could tally out significantly higher.

Conclusion

On July 27, 2012, US President Barack Obama issued
an executive order to implement some of the fixes I
recommended in the previous chapter. He ordered the USCIS
to maintain the longer allowable OPT period (29 months) for
foreign students holding F-1 visas, permitting them to remain
in the United States to work for longer after college. He also
announced that H-4 visa holders—the spouses of H-1Bs—will
receive the right to work without fear of reprisals. Unfortunately,
these are executive fiats and do not hold the force of law. The next
president, or even Obama himself, could reverse these orders
without requiring approval from any other government body.
Furthermore, it remains unclear whether H-4 spouses will only
be allowed to work after the sixth year of the H-1B, and if the H-1B
is entitled to extensions beyond the sixth year based on a green
card filing. "This would be too limited. H-4 spouses should be
allowed to work much earlier—from day one," says immigration
attorney Cyrus B. Mehta. To be clear, I credit Obama and other
legislators on both sides of the aisle for discussing and pushing
forward legislation to improve the lot of skilled immigrants and
allow more of them to stay here and contribute to America.

However, to date no permanent changes have made it
through the US Congress, and this inability to do so illustrates a
simple fact: immigration policy reform is not really a priority for
the US government. Bailing out big banks is far more important.
Funding distant wars of dubious value to the tune of trillions of

dollars is more important. Fundamental yet simple immigration changes that could create a better future for our children and our nation, however, aren't really worth the trouble and the time, despite there being a strong consensus in Washington, DC, that immigration reform is vital to American competitiveness around the globe. In the political equation, immigration reform is a third-rail issue. A few legislators have introduced bills and pushed hard, but the paucity of results speaks far louder than the press releases or the good intentions of a vocal minority.

The skilled immigrants, for their part, have no real voice or influence in the process that controls both them and the destiny of the US economy. Skilled immigrants do not spend millions of dollars on lobbyists. They cannot vote. The communities of their ethnic peers in America, likewise, do not wield significant political clout and do not represent a unified voting bloc. The only advocates for skilled immigrants of any real influence, the large US multinationals that hire H-1Bs and the US Chamber of Commerce, have not made immigration reform a defining issue or a top priority. The only people who care enough to shout from the rooftops are venture capitalists and those interested in maintaining the United States as the leading incubator for startups—people like venture capitalist Brad Feld, LinkedIn founder Reid Hoffman, Netscape co-founder Marc Andreessen, and Google chairman Eric Schmidt. The loudest government voice has been New York City mayor Michael Bloomberg, who has called US immigration policies "economic suicide."

Ironically, the highly accomplished foreigners in our midst who admire America also see the danger we face most clearly. In response to an article I had written about the American brain drain for *BusinessWeek* magazine in April 2009, predicting an American brain drain, Alcoa CEO Klaus Kleinfeld wrote an email of thanks. Getting an email from the CEO of one of the world's largest companies means the right people are reading my columns. Kleinfeld, a German citizen living in the United States, concisely stated what I so often struggle to summarize about why stopping the Immigrant Exodus is so crucial not just to America but to the world as a whole. Kleinfeld explained how the statistics and conclusions I had presented sent a warning to everyone who values the contributions of American inventiveness and entrepreneurial spirit. He wrote:

> Those of us who grew up in other countries and cultures can see and appreciate the power of those unique American values perhaps better than Americans themselves. We are energized by the freedom of opportunity, the dynamic business culture, and the excellent schools of higher learning. We are motivated to use that energy and learning to better ourselves in this land of opportunity, and in the process to contribute to America's success. Down through US history, the competition from succeeding waves of immigrants created the force that drove Americans to excel. It seems to me the US will continue to thrive as long as the best and brightest from other lands continue to contribute to America's progress and compete for its opportunities.

> While a "brain drain" would be tragic for the US, it would also be harmful to the international network of commerce and innovation that has played an important role in global progress and human development. The hub of that network, the engine for that progress, has been the US immigrants and "guests" like myself who bring an international understanding and insights about how the US can continue to fulfill its important leadership role in today's global society.

In this era of rapid globalization, there is no question that Brazil, China, and India will develop quickly, and they will increasingly challenge the United States for technological supremacy. Indeed, this is already the case in key sectors. China has built the world's largest network of high-speed trains, and it leads the world in installation of clean-coal–fired power plants and solar panel production. India has become a core R&D center for many large multinationals, and scientists in the subcontinent develop products in automotive, medical equipment, and consumer electronics segments designed for markets that more closely resemble India than the United States. Brazil is a global leader in small-plane aviation and oil exploration technology.

But none of these countries have come close to replicating the idea factory and entrepreneurial firepower of the United States. And none of these countries, for the foreseeable future, will be able to replicate the ingredients that made America the dynamo that has driven and still drives global economic and technological progress.

To put this more explicitly, a vibrant United States that opens its doors to skilled immigrants will provide a greater benefit to the rest of the world than a closed, shriveling United States because the rules by which the US practices the game of economic development, job formation, and intellectual capital formation grow the global economic pie. And the ethos that drives America's entrepreneurs and inventors, and has driven US policy until very recently, is critically important for the continued development of the global economy.

That ethos is exemplified in the ingenuity, the persistence, and the perseverance of the wave after wave of talented immigrants who have lifted America to ever greater economic and technological heights from one generation to the next, for nearly 250 years. Today, many pundits and observers question whether we are witnessing the beginning of the decline of the American empire. And I submit to you that this may indeed be the case. In alienating and locking out skilled immigrant entrepreneurs and inventors, we have not only blocked the flow of the very lifeblood that built the economic backbone of this great country, we have also deadened the nerve endings that create the next great thing. If we restore this flow, we restore our nation.

Notes

1 Saxenian, AnnaLee. "Silicon Valley's New Immigrant Entrepreneurs." Public Policy Institute of California. http://www.ppic.org/content/pubs/report/R_699ASR.pdf (accessed July 31, 2012).

2 Wadhwa, Vivek, AnnaLee Saxenian, Ben Rissing, and Gary Gereffi. "America's New Immigrant Entrepreneurs, Part 1." Duke Science, Technology & Innovation Paper No. 23 (2007). Social Science Research Network (SSRN). http://ssrn.com/abstract=990152 (accessed July 31, 2012).

3 Wadhwa, Vivek, AnnaLee Saxenian, Ben Rissing, and Gary Gereffi. "Education, Entrepreneurship and Immigration: America's New Immigrant Entrepreneurs, Part II." Social Science Research Network (SSRN). http://papers.ssrn.com/sol3/papers.cfm?abstract_id=991327 (accessed July 31, 2012).

4 "The 'New American' Fortune 500." Partnership for a New American Economy. http://www.renewoureconomy.org/sites/all/themes/pnae/img/new-american-fortune-500-june-2011.pdf (accessed July 31, 2012).

5 "Immigrant Small Business Owners: A Significant and Growing Part of the Economy." Fiscal Policy Institute (FPI). http://fiscalpolicy.org/immigrant-small-business-owners-a-significant-and-growing-part-of-the-economy (accessed July 31, 2012).

6 Headd, Brian. "An Analysis of Small Business and Jobs." Small Business Research Summary No. 359. US Small Business Administration. Office of Advocacy. http://archive.sba.gov/advo/research/rs359.pdf (accessed July 31, 2012).

7 Fairlie, Robert W. "Open for Business: How Immigrants Are Driving Small Business Creation in the United States." Partnership for a New American Economy. http://www.renewoureconomy.org/sites/all/themes/pnae/openforbusiness.pdf (accessed 8/22/12).

8 Rankings were based on factors, including company growth; past success of CEOs, founders, and investors; capital raised; and potential to become publicly traded in the near future. Anderson, Stuart. "Immigrant Founders and Key Personnel in America's Top Venture-Funded Companies." National Foundation of American Policy. http://www.nfap.com/pdf/NFAPPolicayBriefImmigrant FoundationandKeyPersonnelinAmericasTopVentureFundedCompanies.pdf (accessed July 31, 2012).

9 Ovide, Shira. "Microsoft Seals Deal for Social Site Yammer." *Wall Street Journal*, June 26, 2012. http://online.wsj.com/article/SB1000142405270230487030457748 8860890238078.html (accessed July 31, 2012).

10 Anderson, "Immigrant Founders and Key Personnel in America's Top Venture-Funded Companies."

11 Wadhwa et al. "America's New Immigrant Entrepreneurs."

12 Ibid.

13 "Patent Pending: How Immigrants Are Reinventing the American Economy." Partnership for a New American Economy. http://www.renewoureconomy.org/ patent-pending (accessed July 31, 2012).

14 Ibid.

15 Wadhwa, Vivek, Guillermina Jasso, Ben A. Rissing, Gary Gereffi, and Richard B. Freeman. "Intellectual Property, the Immigration Backlog, and a Reverse Brain-Drain: America's New Immigrant Entrepreneurs, Part III." Social Science Research Network (SSRN). http://ssrn.com/abstract=1008366 (accessed July 31, 2012).

16 US Patent and Trademark Office. Patent Technology Monitoring Team. "US Patent Statistics Summary Table, Calendar Years 1963 to 2011."

17 "World Intellectual Property Indicators—Tables and Figures, Country share in total PCT applications." World Intellectual Property Organization (WIPO). http://www.wipo.int/ipstats/en/wipi/figures.html (accessed August 1, 2012).

18 "Entrepreneurs: Cream of the Young Crop." *BusinessWeek*. http://images. businessweek.com/ss/05/10/young_entrepreneur/source/4.htm (accessed July 31, 2012).

19 Saxenian, AnnaLee, and Jinn-Yuh Hsu. "The Silicon Valley–Hsinchu Connection: Technical Communities and Industrial Upgrading." *Industrial and Corporate Change* 10, no. 4 (2001): 893–920.

20 Saxenian, "Silicon Valley's New Immigrant Entrepreneurs."

21 Wadhwa et al. "America's New Immigrant Entrepreneurs."

22 Wadhwa, Vivek, AnnaLee Saxenian, Richard B. Freeman, and Gary Gereffi. "America's Loss is the World's Gain: America's New Immigrant Entrepreneurs, Part IV." Social Science Research Network (SSRN). http://papers.ssrn.com/sol3/papers.cfm?abstract_id=1348616 (accessed July 31, 2012).

23 Wadhwa, Vivek, Sonali Jain, AnnaLee Saxenian, Gary Gereffi, and Huiyao Wang. "The Grass Is Indeed Greener in India and China for Returnee Entrepreneurs: America's New Immigrant Entrepreneurs, Part VI." Social Science Research Network (SSRN). http://papers.ssrn.com/sol3/papers.cfm?abstract_id=1824670 (accessed July 31, 2012).

24 Wadhwa, Vivek, AnnaLee Saxenian, Richard B. Freeman, and Alex Salkever. "Losing the World's Best and Brightest: America's New Immigrant Entrepreneurs, Part V." Social Science Research Network (SSRN). http://papers.ssrn.com/sol3/papers.cfm?abstract_id=1362012 (accessed July 31, 2012).

25 Finegold, David, B. Venkatesh Kumar, Anne-Laure Winkler, and Vikas Argod. "Will They Return?" Rutgers School of Management and Labor Relations. http://smlr.rutgers.edu/will-they-return (accessed July 31, 2012).

26 Finn, Michael G. "Stay Rates of Foreign Doctorate Recipients from US Universities, 2007." Oak Ridge Institute for Science and Education. http://orise.orau.gov/files/sep/stay-rates-foreign-doctorate-recipients-2007.pdf (accessed July 31, 2012).

27 "Still Waiting: Green Card Problems Persist for High Skill Immigrants." National Foundation for American Policy. http://www.nfap.com/pdf/NFAPPolicyBrief.StillWaiting.June2012.pdf (accessed July 31, 2012).

28 "Science and Engineering Indicators 2012." National Science Foundation. http://www.nsf.gov/statistics /seind12/c2/c2h.htm (accessed July 31, 2012).

29 Ibid.

30 Ibid.

31 Salkever, Alex. "Technical Sutra." Salon.com. http://www.salon.com/writer/ alexander_salkever/ (accessed July 31, 2012).

32 Aggarwal, Alok. "India Emerging as the Preferred Career Destination for IITians." Evalueserve. http://www.ibef.org/download/India_ PreferCareerDestion_IITians_060508.pdf (accessed July 31, 2012).

33 Ruiz, Neil G., Jill H. Wilson, and Shaymali Choudhury. "The Search for Skills: Demand for H-1B Immigrant Workers in US Metropolitan Areas." Brookings Institution. http://www.brookings.edu/research/reports/2012/07/18-h1b-visas-labor-immigration#overview (accessed July 10, 2012).

34 Borjas, George J. "Immigration in High-Skill Labor Markets: The Impact of Foreign Students on the Earnings of Doctorates." National Bureau of Economic Research Working Paper No. w12085 (2006). Social Science Research Network (SSRN). http://papers.ssrn.com/sol3/papers.cfm?abstract_id=888287 (accessed July 31, 2012).

35 "Professor Norm Matloff's H-1B Web Page." http://heather.cs.ucdavis.edu/h1b. html (accessed July 31, 2012).

36 Conroy, Donna. "No Americans Need Apply: 100 Want Ads Exclude Americans from US-Based High-Tech Jobs." Bright Future Jobs. http://brightfuturejobs.com/wp-content/uploads/2012/02/No-Americans-Need-Apply-100-Help-Wanted-Ads-Exclude.pdf. (accessed July 31, 2012).

37 US Citizenship and Immigration Services. "Annual Report for Fiscal Year 2008." http://www.uscis.gov/USCIS/Resources/Reports/uscis-annual-report-2008.pdf (accessed July 31, 2012).

38 Ruiz, Neil G., Jill H. Wilson, and Shaymali Choudhury. "The Search for Skills: Demand for H-1B Immigrant Workers in US Metropolitan Areas."

39 Hunt, Jennifer, and Marjolaine Gauthier-Loiselle. "How Much Does Immigration Boost Innovation?" Institute for the Study of Labor (IZA) Discussion Paper No. 3921 (2009). Social Science Research Network (SSRN). http://papers.ssrn.com/sol3/papers.cfm?abstract_id=1329559 (accessed July 31, 2012).

40 Kerr, William, and William Fabius Lincoln. "The Supply Side of Innovation: H-1B Visa Reforms and US Ethnic Invention." Harvard Business School Entrepreneurial Management 09-005 (2008). http://www.hbs.edu/research/pdf/09-005.pdf (accessed July 31, 2012).

41 Ruiz, "The Search for Skills."

42 Jasso, Guillermina, Vivek Wadhwa, Ben Rissing, Gary Gereffi, and Richard Freeman. "How Many Highly Skilled Foreign-Born Are Waiting in Line for US Legal Permanent Residence?" *International Migration Review* 44, no. 2 (2010): 477–498.

43 Partnership for a New American Economy. "Not Coming to America." http://www.renewoureconomy.org/sites/all/themes/pnae/not-coming-to-america.pdf (accessed July 31, 2012).

44 Galligan, Brian, Martina Boese, Melissa Phillips, and Annika Kearton. "Boosting Regional Settlement of Migrants and Refugees in Australia: Policy Initiatives and Challenges." Australian National University. College of Law. http://law.anu.edu.au/COAST/events/APSA/papers/186.pdf (accessed July 31, 2012).

45 Ibid.

46 Partnership for a New American Economy. "Not Coming to America."

47 Ibid.

48 Ibid.

49 "Singapore Employment Pass Eligibility Certification EPEC Singapore License to Job Hunt." Rikvin. http://www.rikvin.com/blog/singapore-employment-pass-eligibility-certificate-epec-singapore-licence-to-job-hunt (accessed October 11, 2011).

50 Wadhwa et al., "America's New Immigrant Entrepreneurs."

Index

J
Jasso, Guillermina, 60
Jin, Jason Gang, 17, 37–39
Johnson, Lyndon B., 30
Johnson-Reed Act, 30

K
Kapoor, Aman, 79
Katsouleas, Tom, 41
Kauffman Foundation, 39, 40, 68
Kellogg's, 21
Kennedy, Edward, 30
Kennedy, John F., 8, 30
Kerr, William, 57
Kerry, John, 77
Khosla, Vinod, 22
Kleinfeld, Klaus, 82–83
Kuck, Charles H., 48, 49

L
labor mobility, 56, 76
Lewis, Michael, 31
Liang, James, 29
Lincoln, William, 57
LinkedIn, 82
Los Angeles Times, 22
"Losing the World's Best and
   Brightest" (Kauffman
   Foundation), 40
Lugar, Dick, 77

M
Maloney, Carolyn, 77
Maptia, 65–66
Massachusetts Institute of
Technology (MIT), 50
Matloff, Norman S., 53
Mayo Clinic, 52, 56, 58
Mayorkas, Alejandro, 7, 19, 27
Mehta, Cyrus D., 48, 81
Menlo Ventures, 7
Merck, 25
Microsoft, 23, 44

MIRALab, 45
Moran, Jerry, 78
Moritz, Michael, 7
Musk, Elon, 22

N
National Basketball Association
   (NBA), 57–58
National Foundation for American
   Policy (NFAP), 23, 42
National Institutes of Health, 56
National Science Foundation, 42, 57
Netscape, 31
The New New Thing (Lewis), 31
New York University, 58

O
Oak Ridge Institute for Science and
   Education (ORISE), 41–42
Obama, Barack, 81
Ohio State University, 47
Optional Practical Training (OPT)
   period, 42, 77, 81
Oracle, 29
"Outstanding American by Choice"
   Award, 7
Owens, William L., 77

P
Parker, Tony, 58
Partnership for a New American
Economy, 22, 25, 69
Penn State University, 40–41
Pfizer, Charles, 22
Pfizer Drugs, 22
Ping Fu, 7
Pishevar, Shervin, 7
Pitney Bowes, 21
PriceCheckIndia, 45
Procter & Gamble, 21
Pyxoft Infotech, 21

About the Author

Vivek Wadhwa is director of research at the Center for Entrepreneurship and Research Commercialization and executive in residence at the Pratt School of Engineering, Duke University; vice president of innovation and strategy at Singularity University; fellow at the Arthur & Toni Rembe Rock Center for Corporate Governance, Stanford University; and distinguished visiting scholar, Halle Institute of Global Learning, Emory University. He has also been a senior research associate at the Labor and Worklife Program of Harvard Law School and a visiting scholar at the School of Information at the University of California, Berkeley.

In his roles at Duke, Stanford, and Emory Universities, Wadhwa lectures on subjects such as entrepreneurship and public policy, helps prepare students for the real world, and leads groundbreaking research projects.

At Singularity University, he helps educate select groups of leaders about the exponentially growing technologies that are soon going to change our world. These advances—in fields such as robotics, artificial intelligence, computing, synthetic biology, 3-D printing, medicine, and nanomaterials—are making it possible for small teams to do what was once possible for only governments and large corporations to do: solve the grand challenges in education, water, food, shelter, health, and security. Wadhwa is an adviser to several governments; mentors entrepreneurs; and is a regular columnist for the *Washington Post,*

Bloomberg BusinessWeek, Forbes.com, and the American Society of Engineering Education's *Prism* magazine.

Before joining Duke University, Wadhwa was a technology executive known for pioneering change and innovation. He started his career as a software developer and gained a deep understanding of the challenges in building computer systems. His quest to help solve some of IT's most daunting problems began at New York–based investment banking powerhouse Credit Suisse First Boston (CSFB), where he was vice president of information services. There he spearheaded the development of technology for creating computer-aided software-writing systems that was so successful that CSFB decided to spin off that business unit into its own company, Seer Technologies. As its executive vice president and chief technology officer, Wadhwa helped grow the nascent startup into a $118 million publicly traded company.

With the explosive growth of the Internet, Wadhwa saw an even greater opportunity to help businesses adapt to new and fast-changing technologies, and founded Relativity Technologies. As a result of his vision, Forbes.com named Wadhwa a Leader of Tomorrow, and *Fortune* magazine declared Relativity one of the 25 coolest companies in the world. In February 2012, the US government awarded Wadhwa distinguished recognition as an Outstanding American by Choice—for his "commitment to this country and to the common civic values that unite us as Americans."

Wadhwa holds a BA in computing studies from the University of Canberra in Australia, and an MBA from New York University. He is founding president of the Carolinas chapter of The IndUS Entrepreneurs (TIE), a nonprofit global network intended to foster entrepreneurship. He has been featured in thousands of articles in worldwide publications, including the *Wall Street Journal, The Economist, Forbes* magazine, the *Washington Post*, the *New York Times, US News & World Report*, and *Science* magazine, and has made many appearances on US and international television, including CBS (*60 Minutes*), PBS, CNN, ABC, NBC, CNBC, and the BBC.

About the Writer

Alex Salkever is a writer and former editor of BusinessWeek.com where he managed technology coverage for the publication. His work has appeared in numerous national and international publications in print and online including *The Christian Science Monitor, Wired* magazine, Salon.com, *BusinessWeek*, and *Inc.* magazine.

About Wharton Digital Press

Wharton Digital Press was established to inspire bold, insightful thinking within the global business community. In the tradition of The Wharton School of the University of Pennsylvania and its online business journal, *Knowledge@Wharton*, Wharton Digital Press uses innovative digital technologies to help managers meet the challenges of today and tomorrow.

As an entrepreneurial publisher, Wharton Digital Press delivers relevant, accessible, conceptually sound, and empirically based business knowledge to readers wherever and whenever they need it. Its format ranges from ebooks and enhanced ebooks to mobile apps and print books available through print-on-demand technology. Directed to a general business audience, the Press's areas of interest include management and strategy, innovation and entrepreneurship, finance and investment, leadership, marketing, operations, human resources, social responsibility, business-government relations, and more.

wdp.wharton.upenn.edu

About The Wharton School

The Wharton School of the University of Pennsylvania—founded in 1881 as the first collegiate business school—is recognized globally for intellectual leadership and ongoing innovation across every major discipline of business education. The most comprehensive source of business knowledge in the world, Wharton bridges research and practice through its broad engagement with the global business community. The School has more than 4,800 undergraduate, MBA, executive MBA, and doctoral students; more than 9,000 annual participants in executive education programs; and an alumni network of 86,000 graduates.

www.wharton.upenn.edu